Seema Mustafa has been a journalist since the age of 19. She has worked in almost all major Indian newspapers and written for many others—*The Pioneer, The Patriot, The Indian Express, Telegraph, Economic Times, Asian Age*—during a long career that has taken her across the globe on assignments. She has covered conflict in Assam, Punjab and Kashmir; communal violence in different states of India; and was the first Indian journalist to cover the first war in Beirut. In addition, she has worked for a couple of years as the National Affairs Editor for the News X television channel. She is presently the Founder-Editor of *The Citizen*, an online initiative.

AZADI'S DAUGHTER

Being a Secular Muslim in India

A Memoir

SEEMA MUSTAFA

SPEAKING TIGER PUBLISHING PVT. LTD
4381/4 Ansari Road, Daryaganj,
New Delhi–110002, India

First published in India by imprintOne 2012
This edition published by Speaking Tiger 2017

Copyright © Seema Mustafa 2017

ISBN: 978-93-86582-22-5
eISBN: 978-93-86582-21-8

10 9 8 7 6 5 4 3 2 1

The moral right of the author has been asserted.

Typeset in Adobe Jenson Pro by Jojy Philip
Printed at Sanat Printers, Kundli

All rights reserved.
No part of this publication may be reproduced,
transmitted, or stored in a retrieval system, in any form or
by any means, electronic, mechanical, photocopying,
recording or otherwise, without the prior
permission of the publisher.

This book is sold subject to the condition that it shall not,
by way of trade or otherwise, be lent, resold, hired out,
or otherwise circulated, without the publisher's
prior consent, in any form of binding or cover
other than that in which it is published.

To all the innocents in jail

Contents

	Foreword by Zoya Hasan	ix
	Preface	xv
1.	The Elephant in the Room	1
2.	A Place in the Sun	18
3.	The Mosquito and the Bed Bug	37
4.	A Journalist and a Woman	52
5.	Politics: A Trial by Fire	70
6.	Nothing in Common	86
7.	A Blow to Secular India	99
8.	'Speak, Your Life Is Still Yours'	113
9.	The Flames of Two Towers	127
10	Why Aren't Indian Muslims Terrorists?	143
11	The Night before a Dawn	157
	Epilogue	175
	Acknowledgments	187

Foreword

Azadi's Daughter is a fascinating account of a bold, intrepid and audacious woman's journey. It is not merely a personal story; it is a political commentary on a secular way of life in the home and in the world. It chronicles the journey of a Muslim girl born into a nationalist and privileged Muslim family in Lucknow. Seema Mustafa's family was closely involved in the nationalist movement and, at the same time, it was steeped in Lucknow's syncretic culture, which makes for an attractive combination of values and lifestyle. The society and family in which she grew up was liberal, enlightened and progressive. As a child she was oblivious to the language of communalism, seeing herself as no different from others. She reminds the reader that even though her family was secular-modern, it was also staunchly Muslim, but it did not allow itself to be limited by conservative interpretations of Islam. A woman of her background was expected to live her dreams and aspirations, and was clearly encouraged to make her own personal and professional choices. The book should set to rest the rampant disquiet about the absence of modernity among Indian Muslims and Muslim women in particular. The reader must be prepared to have old assumptions defied and prejudices turned on its head.

The protagonist of *Azadi's Daughter* is very much the face of modern India, committed to justice and social equality, living life on her own terms fully in accord with the expectations of her grandmother, a renowned freedom fighter and her mother, the first Muslim woman to work as a sub-editor in the *National Herald* in Lucknow. During her thirty-odd years as a journalist, Seema has reported and written on a broad range of subjects. She is especially known for her coverage of the Shah Bano controversy, communal riots, Kargil war, and the Indo-US nuclear deal which she vehemently opposed and for which she had to resign from the *Asian Age*.

Along the way, the seamless secular and professional story is interrupted by disenchantment and frustration during the 1980s and 1990s as she realized that things were not quite as her grandmother and mother believed. This is the beginning of her political activism, which has ranged from Muslim women's struggle for their rights, to anti-communalism, the Indo-Pakistan peace process and, more recently, promoting a dialogue between the political class in New Delhi and civil and political society in Kashmir. In fact, her political activism and the fragility of Indian secularism become inextricably linked in this story. The book is not a chronological history, but an impressionistic commentary—partly on Indian politics, partly on Muslim politics from the standpoint of an activist whose own experiences mirror the discontents of the community with the state and Muslim leadership. What repeatedly emerges from this account is how the 1980s saw

India's secular foundations being shaken as never before. The secular ideology was discredited and Muslims began to lose faith as the whole issue of the status of minorities and majority-minority relations was opened up with the Shah Bano and the Ayodhya controversies. The decision to revoke the Supreme Court verdict in the Shah Bano case by passing the 1986 MWA, denying Muslim women access to civil law in matters of marriage and divorce, and then the mishandling of the Ayodhya dispute resulting in the destruction of the Babri Masjid, has had a profound impact on Muslims and has been a turning point for Muslims and their attitude to the state. The demolition of the Babri Masjid is perceived to be as much a reflection of lack of political will of secular parties, as it was the result of communal mobilization.

Seema Mustafa highlights security issues which remain a major concern for ordinary Muslims. The pogrom in Gujarat in early 2002 was a watershed in the history of independent India. Over the past fifteen years, the reluctance of the party in power and an administration unwilling to make timely interventions to prevent violence has become a central issue of concern for minorities. From the Mumbai violence in 1992-93 to the Gujarat violence in 2002, Hindu-Muslim riot cases have unvaryingly not resulted in conviction and prosecution of the communally guilty. Communal violence, although still a feature of Indian polity, has been supplemented by the more subtle targeting of Muslims as terrorists. While those found guilty of terrorism in the Mumbai bomb blasts of 1993 have been punished through the legal process, those found guilty of crimes against Muslims during the awful riots in Mumbai after the Babri Masjid demolition are wandering around, free.

Convictions of non-Muslim accused are almost negligible. Suspects from the minority communities are routinely denied bail, unlike suspects from the majority community. This process is further increasing communal divisions and reducing spaces for cross-community interaction, besides further fuelling Muslim social, economic and educational marginalization.

The need for a new deal for Muslims, better education and a more equitable distribution of income and resources in the wake of the Sachar Committee recommendations is a matter of great concern; this is a running theme throughout the book, especially since the idea of a new deal has energized Muslims to make claims to a better life. Muslims, like other deprived groups, face multiple challenges relating to security, identity and equity. The landmark Sachar Committee revealed that they lag behind in every aspect of socio-economic development, thus exposing the hollowness of the propaganda that Muslims are being appeased. Their status in contemporary India was not very different from that of the Dalit in the mid-twentieth century, which led to constitutionally mandated affirmative action in their favour. While, on the one hand, it was widely believed that Muslim backwardness was due to their indifference to modern education, on the other, there has been a continued neglect on the part of central and state governments to address the problems of minorities. The underlying inequities are startling. Whichever way we look at it, the Sachar Committee Report provides extensive data to bolster the case for government intervention to rectify the deficit. But this action has not quite happened.

What comes through most vividly in *Azadi's Daughter* is the abiding faith in Indian democracy. Despite the fact that Muslims face discrimination and are worse off than the majority on almost all indicators, India has been fortunate in avoiding Muslim estrangement from the polity. One indication of integration is the negligible number of Muslims who have taken to terrorism. That Muslims have stood up in this way was surely due to the fact that they lived in a democratic and pluralistic society. They have not fallen into the terrorism trap as they have the chance to participate in regular elections and choose their representatives—an opportunity denied to their co-religionists in most parts of the world. They are the only Muslim population in the world to enjoy such a long and virtually uninterrupted period of democracy—sixty-five years. Democratic politics has helped to create a sense of hope and a prospect of advancement through equal citizenship, and minority rights has given them a sense of belonging.

Whilst Muslims are questioning the terms of the protectionist entente between them and the state, the political class is yet to respond appropriately to this new assertion of equality. Seema Mustafa offers a strong critique of the failures of the Muslim elite and Muslim organizations, and their obsession with securing their own interests on the basis of state or religious patronage. As she says, these leaders do not raise a voice over the arrests of the innocent; none of them has been active in dispensing justice in Gujarat, for instance, where many of the major legal battles are being fought by relatives of the victims along with secular organizations. The foot-dragging on the part of the political leadership in coming to grips with deprivation of Muslims would suggest that the prevailing international and national context has an inhibiting effect on the willingness of politicians to chart any new course of action for minority empowerment.

Over the past two decades or so, the Muslim mind has shifted from fear, resentment and uncertainty to a new sense of assertion of equality. Part of this confidence has been gifted to them by the unique democratic values of the Constitution. Much like the assertion of disadvantaged groups, which has taken an organized form since the late 1980s, Muslims have invariably organized around positive demands for economic and political empowerment. Most Muslims, especially the young, are very different today. They are not contented with gestures of protection and patronage because they believe safety and security is their right. Surely, they want to be treated as equals; in addition, they want public goods and affirmative action like the other deprived and disadvantaged groups. Thus, the issues of jobs, education, health, housing and greater political representation have come to the forefront. This is changing the dynamics of Muslim politics as there is a desire to be part of decision-making at the same time as they want justice and equity to be delivered to them.

New Delhi
12 September 2012

ZOYA HASAN
Retired Professor and former Dean,
School of Social Sciences,
Jawaharlal Nehru University

Preface

When I first thought of writing this book in 2012, it was clear that Muslims were feeling the weight of being a minority in India. There was a certain defensiveness creeping in that was not as visible before. Up till then, one had never dreamt, even in the worst of times, that a day would come when the minorities would not be on the inside as equal participants, but pushed outside, at best looking in. Even that window seems to be in danger of closing now, as those pushing it shut in an aggressive display of exclusionary politics are becoming stronger, more confident, more intolerant, and forging ahead while all opposition seems to crumble around them.

I wonder now, in 2017, whether all that one had believed over the years was right. All those lessons in tolerance and secularism; the conviction that India would never change insofar as the basics of inclusiveness were concerned; that the ups would cancel the downs; that Gujarat in 2002, despite the ferocity of violence, was not the norm; that India would struggle her way out of the shadows into the sun yet again…

Times could be bad, they could be good, but even at the worst points there was hope.

I—like so many others clinging on to this Idea of India—had gone into a state of denial. This was never more visible than in early 2017, when I lost my moorings as a journalist in my home state of Uttar Pradesh, while covering the elections. This was the first time in my long years of journalism that, despite being on the ground, I read it wrong. And clearly, now with the wisdom of hindsight, because I wanted to read it wrong.

I alternate between hurt, despair, anger. I wonder whether I have a space left in this new India basing its politics and its future on war and hate; where nationalism has become militaristic; where to speak of peace makes you an anti-national; where to be a Muslim opens you to attack; where dissent is not tolerated and where people have ceased to matter.

I am a Muslim, culturally but not religiously. This is important for those who plan on reading this book. It is an identity that I decided, very consciously, to adopt along the way to help counter the stereotype of the Muslim that was being created by the political parties, and even governments, in India.

I have to confess that being 'Muslim' to my mind is not a big part of my life and experience. It is an identity that I decided to exercise along the way to counter the created stereotype of the average Muslim that seemed to be spreading across India, I have many identities that perhaps define me better in the long run, having had a far greater impact in shaping my life and my beliefs. Two that I can single out immediately are that of being a mother, and a journalist; identities that are not just humbling and permanent for me, but also where in the learning curve never ends.

I find all my identities under threat today. As a woman, as a journalist, as a Muslim, as a secularist, as a liberal and even as an Indian, because the Idea of India as envisaged by those who led the struggle for Independence, and as enshrined in the Constitution with all its guarantees and its protection, is under threat.

As the narrative changed, I started feeling the need to record the story of inclusiveness, of pride, of secularism, of equality and rights—before they disappeared. And perhaps, in one way, to correct the misunderstandings and propaganda, and thereby demonstrate that the Indian Muslim is not the 'other' but part of the 'us'.

Today I wonder have we, as Indians, failed that Idea of India? Or is it that the Idea has failed us?

SEEMA MUSTAFA

New Delhi
May 2017

CHAPTER ONE

The Elephant in the Room

It was the History period for Class IV in the Convent of Jesus and Mary in New Delhi. The topic was the history of Islam. Not a particularly interested student at the best of times, I was delighted to find that I knew something that perhaps others did not and so jumped up to narrate a story about Abraham—except that I had confused him for Prophet Mohammad. So, according to my version, Mohammad was against idol worship, and spent a great deal of time trying to convince idol worshippers to stop the practice. One day when the elders all left for work, he cut off the limbs of the idols and left an axe near the largest idol. When the men returned they were shocked and shouted, 'Who has done this?'

'Ask him, he is carrying the axe,' replied the Prophet (according to my version of the story), pointing to the largest idol with the axe.

'He does not speak,' said the elders.

'Then why do you worship him?' asked the Prophet.

Needless to say the story was full of inaccuracies, the biggest being that it was Abraham and not Mohammad in the factual version. But I sat down, quite happy with myself and not quite understanding the silence in the room. It was broken when a girl I considered to be a close friend, stood up and shouted, 'Well, I wish they had cut off Prophet Mohammad's nose!'

This, I must confess, all happened during a brief 'being a good Muslim' period I was going through—I later became a 'righteous Christian', collecting pictures of Jesus Christ with the same fervour for at least a couple of years. But at the time I was shocked, and controlled my tears with difficulty. I could not wait to get home, and ran to my mother sobbing. I narrated the story, sure that she would understand and commiserate. She listened quietly and when my tears subsided said, 'You know that everyone has their own way of praying and believing in God. The Muslims say their namaz, the Christians go to church and pray, Hindus worship idols as the image of God. Don't you think when you narrated this story, your friend and others in the class thought you were attacking their way of worship?' She left it at that.

I went back and apologized to my friend and we remained friends all through school. This was my first lesson in secularism and one that has stayed with me all my life.

My eldest brother Kamal, now an investment banker in the United States, remembers how he wanted to get out of going to church in La Martiniere College where he was a young student, so he could have the precious free time all hostel students crave. Mass was mandatory for all students, unless the parents sent a letter requesting otherwise. He approached my mother with a considered 'good Muslim' argument that he was sure would work. Instead, he was told, 'They are giving you respect by inviting you to church, you give them the respect of going.' And that was the end of the argument.

I changed from being a devout Muslim at the age of eight years to being a devout Christian. I envied the Christian girls at the Covent of Jesus and Mary who went in their maroon berets for mass every morning, I used every opportunity I could find to go to the Sacred Heart Cathedral next to our school. I would convince my parents to take me to Connaught Place to collect the comic books on Jesus Christ that were given free in those days by evangelists from the West. I got high marks in Moral Science every year, and low percentages in the other subjects. This never became an issue in the family, just a source of amusement with the occasional remark, such as 'Why can't you get the same marks in Mathematics that you get in Moral Science?' We learnt pretty early on that tolerance was the key that saved the religious from becoming fundamentalist.

Secularism inside our home was a way of life. We were never taught to discriminate, or more importantly, to differentiate on the basis of gender or religion. As children we were quite oblivious to the language of communalism, seeing ourselves as no different from the others. The thought that a Muslim name might evoke a hostile reaction was furthest from our minds, as we lived an elite life without any understanding of those who felt the discrimination every single day.

My grandmother, Begum Anis Kidwai, known as Anis Apa to all, including her own children, had overcome a deep tragedy—the murder of her husband Shafi Ahmed Kidwai—by plunging into the fight for freedom with Gandhi. She was a walking symbol of true secularism. She taught us through her own example how to separate religion from politics, and how to ensure that the discipline of religion should not be allowed to intrude into human relations. She prayed five times a day, she kept the month-long fast, but she did this quietly without making a song and dance about it. I remember that one day we were travelling together by train to Alwar, where my father was then posted. The compartment was the old-fashioned bogey with berths for just four passengers. At the appointed time, Anis Apa took out her prayer mat and quietly said her namaz. I looked at the other passengers in the compartment for reactions, but given the fact that she had not stepped on their toes, they, too, ensured her the privacy she sought for those few minutes.

Anis Apa was a Rajya Sabha member for twelve years. Her residence at 16 Windsor Place was host to her colleagues and home to attractive young Muslim and non-Muslim working women. Her closest friends, Mridula Sarabai and Subhadhra Joshi, were in and out of the house. The three had shared long days and nights together during the violence of Partition, trying to organize relief and rehabilitation for the victims. Mridulaji would march in with her short hair and white-bordered sari, and while some adults were wary of her blunt ways, we as children sensed her affection and deep love for Anis Apa, and loved her for it. Incidentally, it was these same three women who showed the courage to meet then Prime Minister Indira Gandhi during the Emergency and protest against the behaviour of her son, Sanjay Gandhi, who had suppressed democratic rights and launched the terrible family-planning drive that was making villagers in Uttar Pradesh flee in fear of their lives. They were hopeful they would be heard when they went there. They returned quietly. I remember Apa sitting quietly in her room and when I asked her what had happened she said in wonderment, 'She (Indira) asked us to go and meet Sanjay Gandhi!'

'And did you?'

'No,' was the quiet response. Her faith in the party she had fought with and for was clearly shattered.

Every now and again, bitten by a qualm of conscience, Anis Apa tried to teach her grandchildren the godly ways, but her sense of humour never deserted her. One day she managed to get hold of me and insisted I should learn to say the namaz. Patiently she went through the prayers, as I mumbled along, and when we had almost reached the end of what was indeed a major effort on her part, she realized that I was chewing gum. It is forbidden to eat or drink while praying. Instead of losing her temper, she dissolved into laughter, and I ran away, happy to be free.

~

We knew while growing up that our grandfather, supervising refugee rehabilitation in Dehradun, had been brutally murdered. But the identity of the assailant was never discussed, and I at least got to know the details only in my young adult years. No one ever spoke of the murder, or the person who killed 'Shafi bhai', as my grandfather was popularly known. The religious identity of the assailant was clearly made unimportant in the family discourse. The reason was more important than the individual, and the reason had been provided by the terrible violence that engulfed India as soon as Partition was announced. The person who killed our grandfather was a victim of the times, as was Shafi Bhai who had defied threats to continue the work of relief and rehabilitation in Dehradun. My grandmother, with three children to bring up, turned grief into an opportunity and joined Gandhi in fighting for a free, sovereign, secular India. When I asked her many decades after, why she had not pursued the matter, and at least insisted on an enquiry she replied, 'I thought of the grief his arrest would have brought to his mother, what was the point, what would I gain?'

My father was a colonel in the army, Lt Colonel Saiyed Mustafa, who had received many medals during his long years with the British Army. He had taken active part in World War II and was full of exciting stories of his journey from Malaysia to Iraq to Egypt and back. In these stories lay lessons of secularism. One of my all-time favourites related to Afghanistan where he was given command of a platoon of Afghan soldiers and on the first day itself realized that rank and religion was not enough to control these proud Pushtuns—he would have to earn their respect. He ordered them to get into battle gear and run with him until they could run no more. He told us how he reached new levels of exhaustion but had to keep going, knowing that if he was not the last man standing he could forget about commanding them. To cut the descriptive story short, he outran all of them. They returned to the camp and exhausted, he was soon in deep slumber. The sound of a man coughing close to his tent woke him up and he looked out to find that they were in the midst of a huge sandstorm. All the tents had been ripped out, but his was still standing because the Pathan soldiers sat holding it down so that he could sleep.

Given his experience, discipline and honesty, we always wondered why he was passed over for promotions in free, independent India. As I grew up, entered journalism and gained a better understanding of the world around, I would question him repeatedly: 'Is this because you are a Muslim?'

'No,' was the answer every time over the years. 'I was too honest for the Army.' One of the stories I remember was how, when posted in Jammu, he took on the senior officers because they had directed the rations supplier to give them better meat than was supplied to the soldiers. When Colonel Mustafa took charge he stopped the special ration supplies to the generals and earned brickbats. He fought the system and paid for it. But never, not even remotely, did he attribute this to being a Muslim. In fact, I remember he was furious when a young distant relative could not get recruited in the Army and stopped by our house in Lucknow to insist that this was because he was a Muslim. Colonel Mustafa would have none of it, and virtually shouted at the relative who beat a hasty retreat. The entire evening my father remained in a bad mood muttering, 'look at that man, puny, undersized…no self-respecting army would recruit him, and he is now giving it all a communal colour.'

At the same time we were told to fight for our rights, and were given the weapon of education to do so. I remember when a lazy cousin insisted that even his application for a job was rejected because 'I am a Muslim.' I refused to believe him and wanted to know what the official had said.

'Well, he didn't say anything, but the manner in which he threw the application aside, made it clear it was not going to be entertained,' he said. My father who was listening quietly to the argument finally intervened, and not very politely:

'You are educated right, you are qualified for the job, so if he was sneering at you why didn't you catch him by the collar and tell him what you are telling us now?'

And yes, that was another lesson that was drummed into our heads. There is no turning the other cheek, do so once, and if any one hits you again, hit back hard. Particularly, if you sense discrimination.

~

After a lifetime in Bombay, Jammu, Alwar and mainly Delhi, we had to leave for Lucknow when my father retired. I, as the youngest sibling who was still to complete her education, was left with no choice but to go with them. My mother Rafia, popularly known as Azadi as her birth symbolized the dream of her family, was clearly concerned about how I would adjust to 'conservative' Lucknow. She insisted on a wardrobe change from jeans to churidar-kurtas. But the problems she had anticipated for her daughter did not arise, as Lucknow had changed sufficiently since her time at the university to accept jeans and T-shirts—but they did occur for her military husband. Never particularly religious, except when he wanted to be for the sake of an argument, Colonel Mustafa made the local maulvis shudder whenever he visited the mosque for Eid prayers. They kept a huge distance, after the first couple of interactions.

I remember one of these vividly. The imam of the mosque got hold of the Colonel just as he was entering the mosque and admonished him about the length of his pajamas. Apparently they were not the prescribed ankle length. The astounded

Colonel looked down at his pajamas, and then into the imam's eyes and told him in so many words that he did not know even the basics of Islam and that he was not fit to head the mosque. 'I have led prayers in the desert in shorts and boots and you are telling me what length my pajamas should be,' he said. The maulanas never bothered him again.

After my mother's early death, my father stood like a rock beside me to 'protect' me from the fundamentalists in Lucknow. His way of fighting conservatism was to be as audacious as possible. He got me a motorcycle that I drove all over Lucknow. I only now realize how astounded the families we interacted with must have been. But given the standing and supposed 'pedigree' of our family in the elite circles of Lucknow, this did not stop them from sending marriage proposals on behalf of their sons. The Colonel insisted that I meet the aspirants in jeans, and joined me in scoffing at them. A few times, when my grandmother and other elder relatives insisted that a particular proposal be considered seriously, my father stopped them in their tracks with, 'Azadi said that she must never be married in a Rajwara family or to a boy who is not a professional.' So I was protected.

Around this time I decided to learn Urdu, but insisted that it be taught by a person who was not a maulvi, as I only wanted to learn Urdu as a language and not be administered lessons in Islam. A student was found (I later found out he was a student of theology), and he started to teach me Urdu. The first few lessons went well, but then he started quizzing me on my understanding of Islam. I told him that this went beyond the agreement, and that I did not want to discuss the religion with him. He brought it up again the next day and I gave a similar response. When he insisted on giving me a sermon about the religion, I told him that if this continued I would have to stop the lessons. The quiet, bespectacled young man threw down the books and shouted, 'I myself will stop. I do not want to teach you. I only came here because I was told, but did not believe it, that there are Muslims like you also in this world.' Needless to say, that was the last I saw of him! It was also my first intimation that Muslims, too, had major problems with other Muslims.

Loreto College in Lucknow was an experience in more ways than one. Other students, used to the conservative stereotype of Muslims, created by communal politicians and politics, and, to some extent, by the community itself, would come up to me all the time saying, 'you are a Muslim but you don't look like a Muslim.' I would invariably respond with, 'what are Muslims supposed to look like, do they have horns?'

But then some of the inquisitors would add, 'why are you people here, why don't you go to Pakistan.' This, again, was a first for me. It was only in Lucknow that I realized how the communal campaign in India based itself largely on the violence and ignominy of Partition, and insisted on linking Indian Muslims who had chosen to remain with the new country. This incensed my normally peaceful mother. 'Tell them we belong here, and if they are so concerned they can make the journey to Pakistan,' she would say.

But at the same time there was an underlying secularism in the streets of Lucknow where Urdu was spoken so beautifully by non-Muslims and where there was a synthesis of cultures in the music, the dress and even the food. A happy tolerance, which pervaded the scintillating city. One ignored the odd voices: the distant aunt whom we heard admonishing her daughter not to make friends with 'Hindus', or the story narrated by a close friend of how her relatives never invited Muslims to eat in their house.

∼

Initially, during my working years in Delhi, I did not face this rather rude, but perhaps honest, 'are you indeed a Muslim' questioning, the 'Mustafa' in my name remaining muted—until the demolition of the Babri Masjid and after. Until 1992, right through the 1980s, I was just a reporter having a great time at the job. Now, looking back, I realize from bits and odds of conversations that I remember from the time that some editors were fairly conscious of my religious identity. But the only one to perhaps 'use' it was an editor of *The Indian Express* who ensured that I was assigned to cover a particularly turbulent period in Aligarh Muslim University. The fallout was far more than I could understand at the time. Even today, I meet those who were students then and who have tried to give me an idea of the impact—good and bad—our coverage had had on the politics of the beleaguered university.

But the demolition of the Babri Masjid on December 6, 1992 was the turning point insofar as my education on this front was concerned. From that time I was flooded with hate mail, nasty threats, most insisting I should go to Pakistan. This branding of the Indian Muslim with Pakistan is perhaps the most ugly legacy of Partition. Certainly, the most insulting. The Muslims who stayed in India did so of their own choice. And their links with Pakistan were the links of divided families, not with the country but with their relatives. Unfortunately, this was misinterpreted, and perhaps deliberately so, as a yearning for Pakistan when, in fact, it was quite the opposite.

My family, like thousands of divided families, was a case in point. Of my father's five siblings, the eldest brother had opted to leave for Pakistan at the time of Partition in the belief that the rest would follow. My father in the British army, his younger brother in the civil services, and their two sisters happily married here had no intention of crossing over, and lived in India with no regrets through the long years. But such was the sensitive nature of their jobs (as an army colonel and a senior police officer) that they could not meet until all had retired. This meeting took place in 1982 in India.

But before that, in 1971, tragedy struck the eldest brother in Islamabad, during the Bangladesh war. His only son, an army officer, was taken as a prisoner of war by the Indian army—for a long time they thought he was dead—and his son-in-law, a naval officer, was killed when the Pakistan submarine *Ghazi* was destroyed by the Indian Navy.

My cousin, whom I had never met, was expecting their first child. The grief was overwhelming. The brothers here shared what the brother there was going through. But their tears were not for Pakistan; they were for a brother's suffering. And for the sudden realization that they could not be there for each other's sorrow, that the eldest brother they had spent half their lives with was left alone to cry. The twist in the tale, of course, was his children were killed and taken prisoner at a time when his siblings in India were celebrating their country's victory. It was then that I understood that one could cry for relatives without caring for the country they lived in, and that the tears shed by Muslim families in India were never for Pakistan but for their relatives across the border. Right-wing forces did not hesitate to communalize this, insisting that the Indian Muslim supported Pakistan, not just during cricket matches, but also during conflict and war. Not a single ordinary Muslim I have met has any longing for Pakistan in his heart. Only for his family, which in his mind is quite disconnected from the state.

Colonel Mustafa visited his brother for the first time after Partition in the late 1990s. It was a short visit, happy and cordial, during which he met all the estranged relatives. He went back the next year, and returned, never to visit Pakistan again.

It was, by all accounts, a disastrous visit. The talk turned to the army and my father astounded the gathering with his observation that 'the Pakistan army cannot fight; its pot-bellied generals have become too accustomed to air conditioners and the good political life to be able to direct their soldiers at all.' He sought to convince the Pakistanis that Partition had been a major mistake, that Indian Muslims were thriving, and that the Pakistan army was no match for the Indian army. To an intervention that the Indians had fed crushed glass to Pakistan POWs after the Bangladesh war he was scathing. 'This is all lies, rubbish. The Geneva Convention was in force, there was no way that the Indian army would or could treat the POWs in this manner.' The silence in the room reminded him that his own nephew had been a POW for 16 months but he was unrepentant. Mustafa returned to India, with a quiet understanding between the two brothers to love and miss each other, but from a distance.

As the years go by the baggage is definitely becoming lighter. Our generation is freer than the Partition generation. Interestingly, when Indian and Pakistani relatives meet, both take care not to raise controversial issues, there is a great deal of skirting around the bush, as the talk focuses on the younger days, pre-Partition stories and other such topics. Neither side criticizes their own country in the presence of the other, and is usually careful not to allow conversations develop into heated arguments. I believe this is because Pakistanis do not want to say anything that might refute the big claim of living happily ever after in a Muslim country, while the Indian Muslims keep their counsel because they realize that their anger about Partition is not shared by their relatives. Our generation is thus, fairly free of the baggage. Many have lost touch with the relatives there and, for both sides, India and Pakistan are two separate countries, with actually not that much in common.

The generations after mine are even more disconnected and I believe that, if Pakistan is able to rid itself of the terror industry and both countries strike highly secular notes, genuine peace and good relations are achievable in the near future. The umbilical cord has frayed to a point where it is going to snap, and at that point, if both India and Pakistan have wise and courageous leaders, peace will become a hard reality.

It is exactly this conflation of Muslim with Pakistani that makes one boil in anger when after every terror attack in India, voices are heard through the media and at New Delhi dinners asking why the Muslims have not stood up to condemn the attack. I remember a former foreign secretary calling me the morning of one such attack and asking, 'why don't the Muslims issue a statement condemning these terrorists? You should tell them to.' I was not very polite in my response and, unsurprisingly, lost touch with the gentleman who went on to become a governor. Why should Muslims have to issue any such statement? Do they own these terrorists? Are they citizens of Pakistan? In the streets of Mumbai the terror attacks claimed both Hindu and Muslim lives. More Muslims than Hindus have been killed by terrorists in Kashmir. These facts and figures are available in all records. So why do Muslims have to jump to attention when terrorists, who know no religion, strike?

~

I realized quite early in my journalistic career that things were not as my grandmother and mother believed. Secularism was not enshrined in the heart and soul of India, and it was taking deep knocks over and over again. The 1980s saw India's secular foundations being shaken as never before. The law based on the 'goodness of man' became redundant as the masks were taken off, knives and daggers picked up to stab, wound and kill. We, as journalists, ran from the East to the West covering communal violence in different parts of Uttar Pradesh and Bihar, and from there the massacres in Assam, and from there to Punjab and then, in 1984, back to Delhi to cover the brutal killing of at least 2,500 Sikhs while the government sat and watched. It was unbelievable as the beliefs of childhood, the faith and the idealism, was destroyed in front of our eyes. Secularism remained just in name as the mobs took to the streets, and with the help of the police, killed the innocent on the basis of deliberate rumours designed to turn men into animals.

But even in this grim scenario, individual examples of humanity remained, as families reached out to help the victims, despite the risk and danger to themselves. I remembered a story that I heard from my second brother, Bobby, about the Partition. He was not born then but had heard it from my parents while growing up. My mother was expecting her eldest son just after the country gained Independence. Violence had broken out in all of North India; the cities and railway tracks were strewn with dead bodies. My father, then a captain in the army, was rushed to Jammu and such was the atmosphere that he decided to take his pregnant wife with him. They were living in small quarters in a building owned by a Sikh landlord. A few days later, my father had to go to the border areas, and he went to the landlord saying, 'I am leaving my wife in your care.' A night later, our mother woke up in the early hours of the morning to the sound of screaming, shouting and terrible wailing. Terrified, she bolted the windows, cowering in her bed. She then heard the sound of heavy footsteps coming up the stairs to their apartment. There was a knock on the door. Almost paralyzed with fear, she managed to look out to see the landlord standing outside. She opened the door, he came in, asked her if she was okay and apologized for the screams and the wails. She asked him what had happened. He told her that every single member of his family—his son, daughter, in-laws and other close relatives—had all been butchered in

Pakistan. 'I just came to tell you not to worry, your husband has left you in our care,' the old man said and left. It was an incident that my mother could never forget.

CHAPTER TWO

A Place In the Sun

Sparkling, beautiful, highly educated women. A grandmother who shed her burkha to join Gandhi and the Quit India movement and never looked back. A mother who was one of the handful of Muslim women enrolled for a Masters course in Lucknow University in the 1940s and who went on to become a sub-editor in the then newly launched *National Herald*. An aunt who fought with the political authorities to bring justice to destitute Muslim woman, and started a Women's Home and a school in her village, Masauli in district Barabanki. A cousin who was known as Marilyn Monroe in the 1960s and defied Aligarh Muslim University's norms to become an outstanding sportswoman of that time. Cousins and aunts who travelled the world, stood shoulder to shoulder with the men, and laughed their way through the deepest adversity; most of them worked, as teachers, as doctors, as engineers. The sky was theirs.

Two families, one the proud, nationalist Kidwai family of Awadh and the other a more conservative family of

Moradabad came together in marriage. Azadi (my mother) led the way into a profession, becoming the first working woman in her entire family. She was under no pressure to tie the knot and had made it clear to the head of the family, a freedom fighter who went on to become a minister in the first cabinet of independent India, Rafi Ahmad Kidwai, that she would marry a person she felt she could spend the rest of her life with. One such gentleman came along in the mid-1940s who seemed to be a definite possibility. But over a few days his remarks suggested a certain fondness for the green bucks that made Azadi reject him even as the families had almost finalized the marriage. Her family accepted her decision without a murmur, as the choice was hers. To cut a long story short, Syed Mustafa, a swashbuckling, handsome army officer came in from a posting abroad, both met over a cup of tea and the decision was made. Mustafa was definitely not stingy, quite the opposite really, with his admiration for the British Army tempered over the years by his mature, and far gentler wife.

Mustafa's sisters were homemakers, but women who encouraged their daughters to study and work. One became an engineer, another a teacher, and a third wound up as the principal of a girls' school in Lucknow. Two cousins did not marry, as they did not find a suitable match; one did and left her husband because of neglect; another remained a homemaker but ensured that her daughters grew up to be highly qualified doctors.

Azadi's cousins, too, were beautiful women, irreverent and full of fun. A cousin who received a talaqnama through the mail refused to be put down and brought home a second husband. When even this did not work, she decided to devote her life to the three children from the two marriages.

And by the way in case anyone is missing the point, all these women were staunch Muslims, said their prayers, observed the rituals—but did not allow themselves to be caged and shackled by the conservative interpretation of Islam.

One of Azadi's many uncles, this one younger than her, spent the 1960s courting a Hindu teacher in the village school. She was a lovely woman, very popular with the family, and while some adults no doubt looked askance, he faced no opposition when he decided to marry her. They lived happily after, with a son qualifying for the civil services, after studying partly in the village school.

Azadi's maternal uncle, Jamal Kidwai, a stunningly handsome man, married an attractive Sikh woman after he ran away from a forced marriage in his youth. As children, we could listen over and over again to the story of how he did not want to marry a family relative, how he developed high fever but was dragged to the altar by the elders even as he clung to walls and furniture. He had a son by his first marriage, and the first wife remained in love with him till the day she died. She smiled her way through the good-natured jokes in the family about her undying love for Jamal. His second wife, too, managed the clan quite well, becoming a close friend of Azadi and her younger sister Kishwar.

~

My maternal grandmother, Begum Anis Kidwai, started her young life in purdah. Clearly she resented and rebelled against this, and at the first opportunity in her adult life discarded it for a life of public service. In her book *Azaadi ki Chaaon Mein (In the Shadows of Freedom)* translated into English by her granddaughter, Ayesha Kidwai, she wrote of her father, dying of cholera at the age of thirty-three:

> 'My mother watched him from afar. My dadi could caress her hands on his head; my phuphi could rest her head on his chest; but the wife, who was losing her all at that moment, had to stand far away, stifling her cries and strangling her emotions.'

Anis Apa had an amazing relationship with her mother that she acknowledges through her book. 'My mother was wonderful… my one ally…,' she wrote. Of how her mother sat cradling her daughter in the days after her husband's death, and how in those days, 'the widow's bed could not be moved until the iddat period was over. She could also not visit her natal home for a whole year.' Clearly, a conservative family where women observed full purdah and existed to serve the men. Apa too conformed at the beginning. She was married early, at the age of sixteen although as she records in her book, she did try to demur and suggest that the marriage could be deferred by another two years. No one heard her, or if they did they did not heed her, as sixteen was not considered early for marriage at the time. She went on to have several children, of whom three survived. And while she lived in intensely political times, she remained a homemaker until her husband Shafi ur Rehman Kidwai was brutally murdered in Dehradun during the violence of Partition.

It was then that Apa broke all norms, discarded the purdah for good and ensured that her children and grandchildren grew up free of the shackles of narrow and restrictive religion. She turned to Gandhi for 'work' that could see her through the terrible days, and plunged herself into the relief and rehabilitation of the victims of Partition. Two of her best friends, Mridula Sarabhai and Subhadhra Joshi, worked alongside Apa, and the three women earned a formidable reputation that made them unpopular with the authorities but extremely popular with the inmates of the refugee camps.

As a Rajya Sabha MP, Apa's residence was home to a large number of women, Hindu and Muslim, who had left their towns to work in Delhi. There was Prema Mandi, this lovely, lively woman who thrilled us with stories of her love for Feroze Gandhi (who married Indira Gandhi). She had a framed photograph of him and till today we cannot say whether the affair was real, or just a one-sided, eternal, committed infatuation. She never married as a result, and even today continues to live on her own. There was Saeeda Apa, a dynamic producer in All India Radio who was living at the time with a partner. She would drive into Windsor Place in a convertible in the 1960s, quite open and honest about her relationship. No one judged her, everyone accepted her, with Apa being a close friend and confidante. There was Salma Ajmeri, from a small town for whom 16 Windsor Place was a refuge. She was in the Persian wing of All India Radio, and spent many a night at Apa's house, chasing dreams of finding a young man and settling down. She did marry late in life, and like Prema, remains even today in love with the man who did not really stand by her.

~

My mother died young, a tragedy in our lives and a major blow for Apa who had lost her husband in tragic circumstances, and now her eldest daughter as well, in a reversal of the cycle of life. Apa never spoke of her husband's murder, but wrote of it at great length. We learnt of her emotions, of the fear and devastation through her book. Apa replaced my mother in my life, and I discovered how progressive and radical she really was. She did not make a fetish of it, but ensured that the women in her family were allowed all possible freedoms, within the limits of honesty, and 'decency.' She quietly held the hands of those struggling, either directly through the Destitute Muslim Women's Home she and Kishwar had opened so successfully in Masauli, or by just extending quiet support when they needed it most. Stand on your feet, be independent, was the message from Apa who herself was a living example of a woman who had gone through struggle and adversity to stand proud.

Kishwar, my aunt, was another example. Feisty, beautiful, she was found early on to have a hole in her heart. She resolved not to marry, and devoted her energies to Masauli, the women's home and education. A single woman at the time, well-educated, with a crackling personality, she showed us through sheer example how to deal with politicians and bureaucrats with great dignity.

She, of course, was far more vocal in her criticism of the mullahs than her mother, and often voiced her disgust with the narrow views and regressive policies of the self-styled custodians of Islam. Kishwar came across victims of Muslim laws that were made discriminatory by the narrow interpretation of the religion, and saw for herself how young women were deserted by their husbands without maintenance, and without a formal divorce so that they could not marry again. Most of them were left after they had borne children, and the man, who usually remarried, discarded both the wife and the offspring. This, Kishwar found, was one of the main causes of destitution for Muslim women. Most of them had been married at an early age, were illiterate, and from very poor families that could not support them and their children. Marriage for them was an opportunity to better their lives, but the desertion left them devastated and completely helpless. Most had children to support as the men took care not to carry any burden as they went on their way. The Women's Home in Masauli took in the destitutes and their children, and during their stay tried to make them self sufficient by learning sewing, embroidery, chikan work and then selling their fares through a network that Kishwar and Apa and their friends established. It was a home away from home, and the women and children who were all sent to school, thrived.

Kishwar worked with single-minded dedication to open a girls' school in Masauli, and to upgrade both the boys' and girls' schools to the high school level. She ensured that a bank opened a branch in the village and the people were encouraged to save. Radical work that put the elected legislators from the area to shame, but such was the nature of these great women that they worked quietly, in the shadows, and died with little to no recognition from the Congress Party that they had always supported with a passion which had our generation arguing with them for hours on end.

The rights of women were, and remain, a major concern. Apa notes in her book,

> 'the stories of distressed girls from East Punjab and wrecked women from this side of the border were identical: the flight with family and neighbours from village to camp, on the police's orders; the beginning of the journey in a convoy to Pakistan; ambush on the way; abduction of all young women during the attack; division of these spoils among attackers, police and army. The Conspiracy transcended borders.'

And how during the relief work in camps she found that many abducted women did not want to return. How she tried to explain the reasons to the family, pleaded for an understanding that never did come. She wrote how it was impossible for the families to realize that the abducted girl 'wondered whether her parents, husband, society would own her again. A deep sense of misgiving and a fear of rejection would drive her to refuse the offer.' Apa, who worked day and night in the relief camps after Partition, regretted that they never had the organizational strength to rehabilitate the women, treat their mental and physical illnesses, and give them relief and succour in a manner she would have liked. She pointed out in her book that while the Jamiat Ulema-i-Hind sent male volunteers to work in the camps, they refused to allow their women to join Apa and the others in this task.

We entered our teens believing we had the same rights as men. At home and in the world. We were taught to believe that there was nothing women could not achieve, and the sky was the limit. There was no purdah, no discrimination in education, no wars over property (there was no property to war over), as the men and the boys in the family were taught to respect their women as equals. Cooking and sewing were not valued as tasks and I remember my mother telling conservative Lucknow families whose women often expressed concern about my lack of domestic skills, 'there is no need for her to go into the kitchen, she will learn when she needs to.' We were encouraged to read rather than cook, although occasionally Apa would do her duty with a halfhearted, 'what will you girls do, how will you feed your families when you get married?' She would then laugh at the various retorts: 'I will not get married', 'I will make sure he cooks', 'I will buy cooked food from outside,' and pick up a book herself to read. After retiring from politics Apa, who could not cook to save her life, started entering the kitchen on occasion to produce namakparas with gourmet pride. One suspects this was more to fend off our 'but you never cooked either' comments, in the hope that the example would motivate these graceless granddaughters to learn the basics of cooking.

Gender justice became part of our lives, through stories, shared values and by example. It was not taught, it was part of our being. Women do not have a religion; they are bonded together in the quest for freedom, independence and justice. As journalists we saw them. Women in Nari Niketans, maltreated and discarded by society. Women in refugee camps, bearing the brunt of the violence in Gujarat, traumatized, helpless. Women in the mohallas of Lucknow, bearing child after child, terrified to opt for family planning lest the local maulvi live up to his threat of not reading the funeral prayers of the women who try to control childbirth.

Women shivering with fear in Kashmir and in Hyderabad and in Mumbai when their young husbands or sons are picked up for questioning by the police. But we also saw the flip side of the coin. Women battling adversity to manage their own lives. Women rushing from pillar to post, knocking on the doors of government to trace their missing husbands and sons, mounting pressure on callous administrations. Women discarding the burkha, seeking jobs to feed their young children, starting life anew.

Discrimination, we learnt early on, was not limited to the poor. As we moved out of the shelter of school years into college we realized that a large number of girls, irrespective of religion, were just biding time to get married. As and when marriages were fixed, there were tears and heartbreak, as many of the young students wanted to study further and build careers but were not given a chance to do so by autocratic parents. A young Muslim friend of mine spent days and nights crying after her marriage was fixed to a Pakistani national. She did not want to leave India, but her father did not agree. I was reminded of the story I heard about my father's sister, a lovely looking woman who was forced into marriage at an early age, against her will by her ageing parents and elder siblings. She was so traumatized by it that she never allowed her daughter to marry. Theirs was a painful story, as the mother sought to keep her daughter—a gorgeous woman with dreams of travelling the world—shackled to Lucknow. She died of illness following two nervous breakdowns. The mother survived the daughter, but never admitted that she might have made a mistake in trying to protect a girl who wanted to live life on its terms, and not her mother's dead-end experiences.

There are so many lovely young Muslim women who have become doctors, professors, scientists but cannot find the right Muslim men today. That is becoming a major problem as the educated Muslim man gets married outside, and the young women who still remain under parental constraints find that the proposals of marriage are from men they could not bear to spend minutes, let alone a lifetime with. In a tacit admission of the times, Muslim families who scoffed at marriage agencies are now going on the internet to find a suitable match for their daughters. But they still do so without announcing the fact, so that no one except the other party knows.

Marriage and divorce rights were a big issue, and remain a big issue amongst Muslim women. After the demolition of the Babri Masjid there was a concerted effort by individuals like Asghar Ali Engineer and Imtiaz Ahmad, and organizations across India to press for reforms from within. The earlier Uniform Civil Code demand by liberals was replaced by one for reform from within as we all realized along the way that the first was an imposition, and an attempt to kill the diversity of India. Imtiaz—then teaching in Jawaharlal Nehru University—took the lead to organize discussions on reform from within on a public platform between Muslim liberals and conservatives. The ulema arrived in full strength at these meetings, but so did the liberals and both probably were astounded with each other's views. The liberals questioned the maulanas' authority to interpret Islam in a bigoted fashion, and insisted that a new, progressive interpretation of the Book was required to give women their due in the world. Losing his temper, a young maulvi screamed at one such interaction in New Delhi, 'Where is the destitute Muslim woman? Show me. I have never seen one and I have travelled everywhere. They do not exist, you people are just making all this up!'

Naturally, not much came of these interactions, except a decision to end the 'dialogue' that was going nowhere. Women's organizations succeeded in part in putting together a standardized nikahnama where the interests of the women were protected.

Apa and Azadi both ensured that as children we spent a great deal of time with the destitute women in the Home in Masauli. We enjoyed going there as, for us, it simply meant that there were more children to play with. And it was only in the 1980s that I realized what an education that interaction was, how it honed our thoughts, and how the stories of violence and fear that we listened to shaped our attitude to women. So when the first test came for our generation in the family we passed with flying colours, not as Muslims, but as men and women who were prepared to fight for the rights of the destitute Muslim woman.

Shah Bano was a destitute Muslim woman who had been divorced by her husband in Madhya Pradesh in 1978. She went through the courts seeking maintenance to meet her basic needs, and to save her from complete destitution. Her case came to the Supreme Court after seven years of her lawyers seeking justice under Section 125 of the Criminal Procedure Code. Under this, all destitute women were entitled to receive Rs 500 a month from their divorced or separated husbands as basic maintenance. This particular clause was in the criminal code to highlight the fact that the Indian state considered it a crime for a woman to become a destitute. The apex court ruled in Shah Bano's favour in a landmark judgement that shook the nation. Women's organizations and liberals were jubilant, but even before they could react, the patriarchal Muslim conservative organizations came out in strong condemnation of the ruling. They were upset with the strong wordings of the judgment but even more upset and worried that the ruling could turn the scales, and make divorce a far more costly affair with the Muslim man now having to maintain the wife.

The Indian Muslim man, taking advantage of the reluctance of the state to dabble in religious affairs at the time, was using his own interpretation of the Sharia to divorce his wife with a 'Talaq, Talaq, Talaq' pronouncement even as he brought in another. He also sought to make it clear that he was not responsible for the maintenance of the earlier wife and any children he might have had with her. So the Shah Bano judgment was indeed historic as it sought to make the Muslim man accountable under the law, and this naturally had the entire orthodox community up in arms. I went into many Muslim homes at that time with women's organizations to find that the women either kept quiet about the judgment, or actively supported it, regardless of their men's views.

Soon, a war was raging with the liberals on one side and the conservatives on the other, and the women in between. We decided to chain ourselves to the gates of Parliament to pressure the government to support the judgment, and did so while the debate was going on inside. Then Prime Minister Rajiv Gandhi decided to intervene and first got his close friend and minister Arif Mohammad Khan to welcome the judgment in a speech that warmed the cockles of secular hearts. But overnight, as the lobbying became terribly intense, there was a change of heart. The then Environment minister, Z. R. Ansari was fielded to oppose the judgment, and completely contradict Khan's assertions the previous evening. Our stunned silence was broken by applause on the streets as Muslim organizations hailed their victory. The government decided to legislate to negate the impact of the Shah Bano judgment and despite the nationwide protests, it brought in and passed The Muslim Women (Protection of Rights on Divorce) Act 1986 to take away the right to maintenance of the Muslim woman. The Act basically put the destitute Muslim woman outside the purview of the Indian Criminal Procedure Code so that she was no longer entitled to the paltry maintenance of Rs 500 that would have prevented her from becoming a destitute.

It became apparent to us as we organized demonstrations and public meetings that the situation was becoming complicated. Hindu nationalist parties had decided to jump into the controversy and lambast the government for 'appeasing' the Muslims. It became a task to separate our platform from that of the right-wing Hindu forces, even as the Muslim fundamentalist organizations attacked us for supporting the Bharatiya Janata Party's policies and arguments. Arif Mohammad Khan spoke on both platforms but eventually went over to the Hindu right. We steered clear of both the sides, but were a small group, easily ignored and isolated. Except for a few brave Muslim women who came out from their purdah and homes to speak for their rights, there were only a handful of liberal Muslim women in the struggle for gender justice at the time.

This rather active push for reforms from within was given up by most progressive organizations after the demolition of the Babri Masjid and the realization that the fight had become uglier, and bigger, and that it would now be impossible to make conservative Muslim households listen to a gaggle of women talking of reforms in the religious law. The stepping back was strategic, but necessary. And in the long run, it has worked for the Muslim woman who is slowly but surely coming into her own.

Simplistically put, there is a strange kind of division within the Indian Muslim community on the role of women. In the more educated, liberal and perhaps even elite families, women are given all opportunities to succeed in life. They are educated, they are treated at par with men, they are allowed a say in their marriage, they are encouraged to work, they have a share in the property and as a rule they are given their space under the sun. In the more conservative families, women are treated at par with men inside the house, but are not encouraged to work. In the hard conservative families, they are treated shabbily under the cover of religion, with local clerics interpreting Islamic law to favour a stern, exploitative patriarchal system.

The movement for reforms within the Muslim law, thus, was targeting the last two categories to ensure that the more conservative families did not fall prey to the religious sanctions imposed by the hard conservatives. The educated, liberal woman generally remained out of such controversial issues and it is only in the last ten years that I have noticed a few more stepping in to actively speak on issues concerning their community. Unlike in the 1980s, when very few liberal Muslim women were willing to join us at the meetings supporting the Shah Bano judgment, many more come forward now to speak out against the denial of their fundamental rights.

Muslim women have become more assertive, and more aware of their rights. More and more girls are insisting on education, on the right to employment which has also become an economic necessity, and more importantly, the right to having a say in their marriage and divorce. This is not to say that the change is widespread, but to point out that there is a growing awareness and a desire to strike out for a better life.

Fatwas continue to be pronounced by local clerics to constrain Muslim women. A young woman with five children was deserted by her husband for a second wife in Lucknow. She had no family support and came to Delhi to look for a livelihood. Asked why she had never practiced family planning, she said that the local cleric had declared that he would not read the funeral prayers of any woman found to be taking the help of birth control measures to control the size of her family. The pressures on uneducated Muslim women are too many and too complex to fully understand. But more and more women are getting out of the stranglehold of local clerics who are not educated enough to interpret Islamic law in a modern and progressive fashion.

Interestingly, while the hijab has become more common in Pakistan and West Asia, it is not so in India. More and more women are shedding the burkha to study and work. Even in families that insist on the full veil, young girls take it off when they can. It is viewed by most Muslim women as cumbersome and constricting, and definitely not as a 'protection' against society at large. In most families purdah is confined to the older generation, with the younger women rejecting the veil and the hijab.

I have always wondered what it would feel like to be under the black veil favoured by very conservative Muslim women across the world. How closed and shackled they must be feeling, I thought, how oppressed. I decided to interview them in different places: Lucknow, Iran, Egypt and Pakistan—and found strikingly different responses.

A woman from a reputed family in Old Lucknow looked at me, aghast. 'I have never felt constricted in the burkha, I have never known anything different.'

'But are you saying that because your family brought you up in this manner?'

'What a stupid question', she said, and actually she was right. It was rather silly. The answer went as expected, 'Obviously my parents wanted me to wear the burkha, and they were right. And neither I, nor my daughters for that matter, have ever regretted it.' The family strictly maintains the division of 'zanana' (women) and 'mardana' (men). I did not meet her daughters but did meet many other young women studying in colleges in Lucknow in the 1980s. Those whose families insisted they should drape themselves in the black veil, would take it off as soon as they were inside the gates and revel in their 'freedom.'

In Egypt, the black veil can be seen in the conservative rural areas, but in Cairo for instance there was a time till the late 1990s when the hijab was rarely visible. By the turn of the century it was more common than not and I recall my conversation with two working women, both good friends, with one wearing the hijab and the other not. They had a simple explanation.

'I wear the hijab, not because of religious reasons, but because I feel more secure. Men here give you more respect now if you are well covered, and become quite menacing sometimes if you are not,' said one.

The other without the hijab was as categorical, 'I cannot stand it. And I refuse to become what these men want us to be. I don't know though whether I will have to wear one tomorrow, but I will try to be the last woman standing against this repression.'

In Iran, the young women seem to make up for the veil with makeup and trendy clothes. At a small party, I met several young women who removed the burkha as soon as they walked in. Smoking a cigarette and sipping wine, one of them admitted that she hated the dress, and made sure she accepted only those invitations where she could take it off, even if for a few hours. But on the roads the covering has to be complete and while we, as Indian women, were spared the full veil, we had to wear long-sleeved kurtas with the dupattas draped over her heads to ensure that not a strand of hair was seen. I was told that we were fortunate to be visiting at a time when the law enforcers were a little more relaxed, and we could get away with a lighter drape than usual. Earlier, our hosts informed us, a visible strand of hair could land a woman in trouble. A fellow journalist relaxed to a point where she was walking the streets with us, her dupatta barely covering her head. Within minutes, a group of women police surrounded her, draped the cloth tightly around her head, and made it clear that she should follow the laws.

In Pakistan women are particularly free, trendy and beautifully dressed and made-up. Like Indian Muslim women, they are free of such shackles, and so one was surprised to find a young journalist wearing the hijab in Lahore. She seemed to be particularly progressive in her views and was preparing to marry a non-Muslim from another country. So why the hijab? Again, the reason was far from religious. 'I live on my own in Lahore and it is not very common for a woman in Pakistan to do that. So I find that if I wear the hijab I get more respect, and people tend to leave me alone,' she said.

In India, despite the fact that in conservative households women do veil themselves, there is a noticeable difference between the 1980s and the start of the new millennium. Muslim women in India have started charting out their own path. With little to no help from organizations like the Muslim Personal Law Board (MPLB), they are imbibing ideas of progress and development to change their own lives. The male-dominated MPLB has, in fact, been resistant to change, and even the odd woman member it has accommodated in recent years has supported the men in the narrow interpretation of Islamic laws. It is interesting to note that a Woman's Personal Law Board was started in Lucknow and presented a more reasonable, and at times, even progressive, interpretation of the laws governing Muslim women and their life. But Muslims live outside these boards, and Muslim women in particular are keen to move forward. More and more girls are opting for vocational courses and higher education, with families coming under increasing pressure to open the doors and let their girls out.

As they say, water finds its own level, flowing around obstacles and wearing them with time. This is what the Muslim woman in India seems to be doing. Flowing around the obstacles of law and patriarchal prejudice, and finding her way into the sun!

CHAPTER THREE

The Mosquito and the Bed Bug

'Are you Shias or Sunnis?'

The question jolted me and my cousin Sonia out of the world of books, where wrong did not exist, where the good people always won, where idealism was so rosy that existence did not matter, to look at the questioner with surprise. 'Are you talking to me...' would have been Robert de Niro's words on our lips, had we of course, been older and brasher. But we were just in our teens, and stared vacantly at the young woman who had spoken to us, while our minds grappled with the possible answer.

She was running a small library in Delhi's posh Greater Kailash, and we certainly did not expect the query. She—we never did find out her name but now I guess she too was a Muslim and was trying to slot us into some kind of stereotype—repeated the question. We fumbled and mumbled, whispering to each other, 'who are we?' And then we decided we must be Shias, so we turned to her and rather triumphantly announced, 'Shias.'

The look on her face was of a teacher who had caught you with the wrong answer, so we turned back to the books, suddenly unsure of ourselves. I would have let it go, but Sonia, always more exact, whispered, 'have we said the right thing?'

'No, I think we were wrong, perhaps we are Sunnis?' I whispered back.

And we turned to her and said, 'No, actually we are Sunnis.' By then she had slotted us and seemed least interested in the answer. Obviously, we were ignorant, ill-brought-up girls from Muslim homes that did not care to educate us about the divisiveness of religion, and so certainly not worth wasting time on.

I was fourteen years old and Sonia two years younger. We knew we were Muslims, but had no idea what or who a Shia or Sunni was. We went back and learnt that indeed there were two main types of Muslims, and we were Sunnis. We got some details from our parents and grandmother about the intricate differences between the two, and came quickly to the conclusion that all this was a result of power politics, and had little to do with the religion as such. But why didn't they tell us? And I still remember by mother Azadi's response: 'What difference does this make, you are a human being and an Indian and a Muslim and a woman so why do you want to get branded with small little labels?'

Why indeed? That is a question I have asked myself often since then and one that kept repeating when I walked through the violence-hit streets of Lucknow, covering riots between Shias and Sunnis many years later. I reported the violence, and the arguments given by the leaders of both communities. They did not make sense to me then, they do not make sense to me now. It was clear that the people were being instigated to kill and wound each other by political mullahs who were basically fighting a turf war using religion as the excuse. The anger, the frustration, as the mobs ran rampant and attacked each other was an eye opener. How much they hate each other. Or do they really? Why?

After the incident in the library our ears had become sensitized to the terms. The little frown on a distant relative's face was explained, as her son had decided to marry a Shia girl. One heard the adults discussing the marriage saying, 'well she is nice, even if she is a Shia.' The odd comment from an ageing uncle, 'what do you expect from them, they are Shias after all.' The dismissive tones, the intolerance, it was all there when we decided to look out for it.

I went to Lucknow for college, and it is there that I got to know how the 'khatmal' (bedbug and local word for Shia) hates the 'machhar' (mosquito and a similar insulting word for Sunni) and vice versa. And how the two can never mix. Shias and Sunnis went to different mosques, prayed differently, at different times, and while being the same, worked hard to convince themselves that they were different, and somehow better than the other. Shias and Sunnis could not easily marry each other, this being almost as prohibitive in Lucknow families as marrying outside the religion altogether. Both sides cherished little stories of ridicule about each other, and negated the rich history of Avadh and the region through this petty hatred and intolerance. And when the hate and the anger could not be contained any longer, it burst into violence on the streets of Lucknow, under the careful guidance of the community leaders and their political mentors, pitting the two communities against each other, over and over again.

It became imperative for me to go into history and see if the reasons for the continuing feud, not just in India, but in Pakistan, in Iraq, between Iran and the Arab world, could be justified. The original split took place, knowledgeable adults said, soon after the death of Prophet Mohammad, in the year 632. One group of his followers wanted the Muslims as a community to determine his succession. Another group insisted that it should be someone from the family, and their choice was Ali, the husband of Mohammad's daughter, Fatima. The first group prevailed, and they chose a successor as a community to be the first Caliph. Ali was the fourth Caliph, but a violent war broke out, and two earlier Caliphs were murdered. From the ashes emerged the two groups of Sunnis and Shias, who have remained at loggerheads, and have been used by Imperialist forces for their own ends, ever since. Of course my feeble question, 'why did they not settle on Fatima, the Prophet's daughter instead?' was ignored by the adult narrating this history.

The war continued with Ali's son Hussein leading the Shias. He rejected the Caliphate, he stood up to the Caliph's army and the story goes, he and seventy-two members of his family were killed. Hussein was decapitated and his head was carried in tribute to the Sunni Caliph in Damascus. His body was left at the battlefield in Karbala in Iraq and buried there. I remember, during a visit to Iraq just before the US invasion of that beautiful country, a journalist friend left us in Baghdad to rush away on a visit to Karbala. He said he had been there any number of times, so I asked why he needed to go there again, when he could have instead accompanied us to Northern Iraq. He looked at me strangely before walking away. Now I realize that he thought I was speaking like a Sunni, dismissing his faith, when I was actually only speaking like a journalist wondering why he was spending time on faith when the visit was all about news.

~

Over the years, the Sunni-Shia hatred seems to have subsided in India, but the common understanding for this is that more important issues and insecurities have overtaken the Muslim community as a whole in this country. However, in Pakistan and more specifically in Karachi, Shias continue to be targeted by extremist Sunni groups, with the divisive politics of hate suiting all the vested interests and political parties operating there.

According to a demographic study done by the Pew Research Centre* in 2009, the top five countries with the highest Shia population are Iran (66–70 million), Pakistan (17–26 million), India (16–24 million), Iraq (19—22 million) and finally, Turkey (7–11 million). It is important for countries with a majority Sunni population to protect Shia minorities. In Pakistan, the regular violent attacks on Shia congregations seem to be justified by the inherent prejudice and hatred that characterizes relations between the two groups, with the response to this violence from the Pakistani state and political civil society remaining non-existent or subdued at best.

---

* *The Future of the Global Muslim Population Projections for 2010–2030*, Pew Forum on Religion and Public Life; Pew Research Centre Publications; January 2011.

The Shia-Sunni conflict, like the Hindu-Muslim conflict in India, is all about power. It reflects a power struggle between politicians and vested interests, who prey on prejudice and discrimination, and convert this into violence. As scholar Asghar Ali Engineer points out in *My Quest for Peace, Harmony and Socia Change*,

> 'among all sects of Islam we see huge establishments have come into existence and there is always conflict between various sects, less on account of theologies, beliefs and dogmas but more on account of politics of control of these establishments. Then fatwas declaring each other kafirs fly at each other and some selective Quranic verses or a hadith are conveniently quoted to establish the "truth"of one's sect.'

He goes on to say,

> 'This paradigm shift from khilafat to mulukiyyayt [that is, from deputizing for the Prophet to building a dynastic empire] changed the very basis of Islamic society. It was this paradigm shift which not only established monarchy in Islam—something one does not find either in Quran or Sunnah—but also made the history of Islam bloody and violent. It was this paradigm shift which brought about the gross misuse of concepts like jihad...it was this paradigm shift which made Islam a religion of sword rather than religion of peace.' Engineer urges all Muslims to come together to revert to the genuine spirit of Islam where 'genuine martyrdom is not to kill but to get killed for upholding certain principles and values enshrined in Islam.'

Perhaps this is one of the main reasons why in our house no one spoke of being Shia or Sunni. Faith was very personal, and never taken to the streets. My mother, an idealist committed to the freedom struggle, and my father, a prototypical army officer full of exciting stories of World War II, did not have the time or the inclination to drum the narrow aspects of religion into our heads. My mother prayed often; my father prayed only on Eid but was a strong believer (or at least believed he was); both were good people who did not allow religion to intrude into human relations.

'So how are Shias different,' I asked my mother.

'They are not,' she replied, 'we are all the same.'

'Then why do Shias and Sunnis fight and kill each other?'

'Because they are misguided and ignorant,' she said. And then added, 'because they serve interests they don't even know they are serving.'

I saw this myself during visits to Lucknow and Uttar Pradesh as a journalist. The clerics of both communities being solicited by political parties, being urged to give fatwas or at least some such diktat asking their people to vote for a particular politician, or political party. *Maulanas on hire*, we used to laugh, *Get two for the price of one!* They would crowd iftars hosted by political leaders, they would campaign house to house for them, they would give legitimacy to those who had long since destroyed their secular credentials by campaigning for them, they would even attend birthday parties of top politicians in Delhi in abject displays of Muslim support. They still do, both the Shia and Sunni clerics united in the politics that worked to divide the people and place them on the firing line.

But then, as I spent more and more time in Uttar Pradesh, I realized there was another side to the story—a sad side that required understanding. The maulanas were children from poor homes, sent by their parents to madrasas to avail of free religious education. 'At least they will learn something,' the parents told us in the villages of Eastern Uttar Pradesh where primary schools were in short supply till the 1990s, regardless of government claims. I soon realized that while entering any village with a high percentage of Muslims one only had to look at the children to know whether there was a school or a madarasa in their village. Those with no access to education were half-clad, rowdy, disturbed and virtually out of their parents' control. Those who were going to school or a madarasa were better dressed, cleaner and definitely more restrained. The difference was stark. I realized that the maulanas came from such homes, grew to recite the Quran by rote, did not really understand it, and went on to become clerics, who got respect, if not much money. The money came via political parties for those who were more ambitious and greedy, and that is why one could almost see the jostling for political recognition. Significantly, there was no difference between the Shia or the Sunni clerics here, bonded together in avarice and need.

My grandmother had decided early that she would ensure that her grandchildren at least read the Quran and got some education in Urdu. Given the fact that our parents had admitted us into convent schools, she decided to rely on the maulanas to complete our education. At the time, my cousins and I were living with her at 16 Windsor Place in New

Delhi, a beautiful bungalow allotted to her as a Rajya Sabha Member of Parliament. The worst time of the day for us was when 'Maulvi sahab' would arrive. I must make it clear that we went through a large number of Maulvi sahabs, and now when I look back, it was probably because the four of us were quite a handful. One Maulvi sahab would sleep as we recited whatever we thought the letters spelt, and finally we tied him up under my supervision and fled. We never know how he got loose but we never saw him again. Another came only to eat, and we soon learnt that if we could persuade the family cook to treat the Maulvi sahab to some nice delicacies everyday he would not be particularly concerned about our progress on the Arabic front. Suffice it to say that two years and several Maulvi sahabs later we emerged from the prolonged exercise as educated in Arabic and Urdu as we were when we started. But now, I realize that one's lack of sleep was due to the tensions of supporting a family with little money in hand, and that the other was not greedy for food, but just purely hungry. Hunger affected both the impoverished Sunni and Shia clergy, a fact they refused to recognize when it came to waging war for a history long past.

By not acquainting us with the intricacies of this age-old conflict, perhaps our family tried to protect us from divisive Muslim politics, but in the process they deprived my generation of a needed insight into this complicated relationship. It was more than just prejudice, it was hate that had fostered many conflicts. Even at the time of writing this there has been yet another bomb blast in Karachi, Pakistan, targeting the minority Shia community. The Iran versus Saudi Arabia conflict has historical and contemporary dimensions, with both countries aggressively espousing the cause of Shias and Sunnis respectively, across the world. There has been little effort by any country, or any Muslim organization, to make them bridge this gap, which actually feeds into imperialist plans for the Middle East. For instance, it is no secret that when pulling out of Iraq, the United States had to make peace on this front at least with 'terrorist' Iran, whose influence on the Shia community in that strife-torn country now is well recognized.

These politics, seeping through the Shia-Sunni relationship, are being exploited by vested interests and far more powerful players than the two Muslim sects. This is true not just on the world stage, but also in India, where Lucknow remains the seat of this hatred. There have been some efforts after 9/11 and the US-led crackdown on Islam and Muslims, to unite the two sects, but these still remain fragile and subject to the vagaries of time. The almost historical meeting between Iranian President Mahmoud Ahmadinejad and Saudi Arabia's King Abdullah in December 2007 had just a momentary impact, with relations having soured considerably since then. So much so that Pakistan President Asif Ali Zardari was told rather sternly by King Abdullah not to attend a Terrorism Conference being organized by Iran in June 2011. Zardari did not listen and attended the meeting.

In India too there were some attempts to bridge the gap. Shia Scholar Kalbe Sadiq played a major role, along with Sunni leader Maulana Ali Mian, and their efforts to get both communities to say their prayers together bore some fruit in the initial stages. Both sects issued joint statements against terrorism and bomb blasts in Delhi and did not hesitate to denounce the now dead al Qaeda leader Osama bin Laden on different occasions. 'A terrorist defiles the Quran every time he claims to speak or to act by it, or tries to justify inhumane conduct by making false and baseless claims of divine sanction. He insults Islam by his claim to being Muslim. He disgraces the Muslim brotherhood by claiming to be part of it in any way whatsoever. The likes of Osama bin Laden, and members of the various "Lashkars" and "Millats" who claim terror as their creed would be summarily executed in any court of Shariah (Islamic law)', said one such statement signed by clerics and professionals of both sects.

As a journalist, I had realized while covering the sporadic Shia-Sunni violence in Lucknow that the hatred had been almost institutionalized by the clergy and by politicians who were fearful of a united Muslim constituency. The route of the Shia procession during Muharram in the Old City had become a major bone of contention and in 2005 the two sects clashed, leaving at least three dead, and several injured. This bout of violence brought the attempts to forge Shia-Sunni unity to a quick end, with both groups going back to the comfort of their confrontationist positions. The Shias floated their own All India Shia Muslim Personal Law Board, as a counter to the All India Muslim Personal Law Board (AIMPLB), alleging discrimination within. Shia scholar Kalbe Sadiq remained in the AIMPLB but subsequently addressed a meeting of the Shia Board in 2011 where he said categorically, 'they neglect us.' The Shia Personal Law Board has been asking for separate reservation for Shias, as against the growing demand for Muslim reservation.

Politicians, of course, are never far behind when it comes to Muslim politics in India. In Lucknow, the Hindu nationalist Bharatiya Janata Party has made common cause with the Shia community in a bid to divide the Muslims further. The RSS has been in fairly regular contact with Shia clerics, one of whom, Maulana Hammedul Hasan, declared that he saw nothing wrong in singing the national song *Vande Mataram*, just after the Darul Uloom Deoband had issued a diktat asking Muslims not to sing it. The newspapers reported at the time that Hasan's statement followed a meeting between him and RSS chief K. C. Sudarshan. The Congress claims to deal with Muslims per se and not sects, but the Sunnis get the plum share of party seats and positions, leading to considerable discontent amongst the Shias. It is no secret that the party caters unabashedly to Sunni sentiment when there is a conflict of views, and uses clerics to get votes during the elections. As reporters, we have all witnessed jeep loads of maulanas being taken around by local Congressmen to campaign for the party during elections. Interestingly, in 2010, the Congress in Uttar Pradesh realized that it had lost the Shia community. To regain the lost support it decided to take out a yatra from Hussainabad (the seat of Shia-Sunni conflict) to honour Shia martyrs. The BJP, in a policy decision, decided to woo Shia leaders, in a continuation of the 'divide and rule' policy, and even today insists that the Shias vote for them in Lucknow and other parts of Uttar Pradesh.

Another gimmick to win over Muslim support are Iftar parties. Politicians of all hues, including senior leaders of the BJP, hold Iftars during Ramzaan, inviting a host of Muslim clerics to break their fast in the midst of politicians, journalists and others. If elections are around the corner, the spate of Iftar parties rises considerably, as clearly the Indian politician believes that the way to a Muslim vote is through the maulana's belly!

Fortunately, our families did not have much truck with maulanas, with their role being restricted to weddings and deaths. The emphasis remained on the poor, and not the religious, with charity most on display during the month of Ramzan, when food would be sent everyday, or definitely every Friday, to the local mosques for the poor. Old clothes were also sent to orphanages. On Eid we, as children, accompanied the men to the Jama Masjid in Delhi for prayers. It was a big fun outing, even though we were placed in special enclosures for women. Now, when I look back, I realize that it was an attempt by my grandmother and other elders to claim a space for women in the mosque, even if it was behind curtains. At least we were there, present in a space that has been taken over by Muslim men almost entirely.

Even at weddings, maulanas were not encouraged by our elders to give long sermons, but just to perform the basic service, eat and depart. My maternal family did entertain one Baba Neem Karoli who would appear every now and again to offer prayers and counsel to all who found peace in his views. I never met him even as a child, only heard that he had come, or gone. Astrologers too were kept away, except by a grand uncle who encouraged one such person to visit his residence and tell him good things about his future. My parents happened to be visiting when this gentleman was there, and he insisted on coming to our house. Not wanting to be rude, my father told him to write down his predictions for me (I was just seven years old then). Incidentally, I was told this story when I was an adult. So, this man came, bringing an annual chart of my future. When he came to my fourteenth year, he fell silent.

'Go on,' said my impatient father.

'This is it,' said the man.

'What do you mean "this is it"? Carry on!' shouted my father.

'This is the end,' said the man clearly waiting for some histrionics, money and the rest to extend my life accordingly. He did not reckon with my father, an army man, who caught him by the collar, abused him, and told him to get out of the colony and never show his face there again. That was the first and last astrologer to enter our house.

My own personal encounters with maulanas have not been particularly happy. I went to interview the elder Imam of the Jama Masjid as a young reporter in Delhi and was incensed to find a board outside the imposing structure saying that women were not allowed inside. This was sufficient to make me march in, protesting furiously. Since I was a journalist I was allowed this little eccentricity, and when ushered into the presence of the Imam, gave vent to my feelings of discrimination. He heard me out, but offered no acceptable argument beyond a 'no, no everyone is allowed.' He smiled at this gesticulating, angry girl in jeans and a scarf, more amused than angry.

My other close encounter with maulanas was when my father died. I had to organize the rituals, and in the absence of elder counsel, went to the local mosque in Delhi for help. One would have thought that in death these people would be a little more generous and sympathetic, but we had to run from pillar to post to get a resting place for my father, to keep paying the maulanas money as they were at the door every other day on one pretext or the other. While I insisted on sending money and clothes for a Muslim-run orphanage, they were more interested in receiving cash than kind. One imam started calling my residence at odd hours asking for money, while another only showed his face to remind me that money 'for the mosque' would help my father's soul rest in peace. At the grave, the gold diggers arranged by the imams performed after discussing and finalizing the money they would be paid. The only breath of fresh air was the innocence of the little boys who recited from the Quran, rocking back and forth under the sharp eyes of the elder accompanying them. But there was no joy in their eyes, just a silent resignation. The elder with them was not interested in the food we had prepared for the young boys (which they loved), only in the money he had insisted on—'for the orphanage' of course! It took me several months to get rid of the lot, and find peace in my own lack of faith.

CHAPTER FOUR

A Journalist and a Woman

'Oh you are the journalist who called me, really?' exclaimed a rather surprised looking Mansoor Ali Khan Pataudi at a five-star hotel in Lucknow, bringing the pedestal I had created for him several notches lower. It sounded, to my untrained ears, just like the 'But you don't look like a Muslim' remarks that made my ears ring when I first came to Lucknow for graduation. Perhaps worse, as I idolized Pataudi and expected him to at least recognize me as a journalist, particularly as in my idealistic mind my profession was written across my forehead in bright colours.

I had joined *The Pioneer* even before my graduation results were out, hounding the industrialist proprietor for days and weeks, until he agreed to employ me without pay. I did not care, as I was finally a journalist and that was all that mattered in those heady days of idealism and dreams. And in the process, I had fulfilled an ambition that had grown steadily since I was fourteen years old.

So Pataudi's remarks came as a bit of a surprise to me, because even as a fresher I thought no one could mistake me for anything but a journalist. But later when I look back, with years of grinding experience behind me, I realize that he was responding to the fact that I was a woman, and a Muslim woman, in jeans and a T-shirt in conservative Lucknow. It was a reaction that never really impinged on my consciousness at the time, but probably did define people's reactions to some extent. But at the time, and for at least some years after, I lived in my self-created cocoon and never felt different from any other as I dashed around covering murders and robberies.

The Patriot in Delhi was my first real job, and I became part of a family with one of the best editors I have worked with: Edatata Narayanan, the head, supported by the gentle and beautiful Aruna Asaf Ali. The two years I spent there—leaving only because Narayanan had died and was being replaced by the wily R. K. Mishra—helped strengthen the cocoon. The atmosphere was purely secular, the politics progressive, and the 'Mustafa' in my name was totally inconsequential to my performance as a reporter. I did learn that a surname could be used to good advantage from a colleague though. Kashmiri Pandits at the time were in top gear in the government, and so we often heard him calling highly placed government officials and giving his name with sufficient pomposity as 'Kaul' that personal assistants would scramble to connect him to their boss. And as all journalists know, half the battle is won if a connection is made.

My next stop was *The Indian Express* which allowed me to hone my skills, giving full freedom along with the exposure. An array of editors kept us in check—from the rather imposing Mulgaonkar to the irreverent Kuldip Nayar and the intense

Arun Shourie—even as we were allowed to follow our nose into the most impossible of places. The first hint that I was not seen as just another reporter came when I was actively covering the dirty politics that had come to define the Aligarh Muslim University in the 1980s. Shourie was taking a great interest in the coverage, and a couple of professors at AMU who were at the receiving end of some of my reports spoke of my being used by the *Express* 'just because you are a Muslim.' I dismissed the allegation with all the contempt it deserved, and still do not fully believe that being a Muslim had anything to do with the assignment. For one, I went to AMU at my own initiative as it interested me. And I did follow my nose. Perhaps the display and editor Arun Shourie's interest in my reporting was a little out of the ordinary, but the atmosphere was secular—and fun, as it was a reporter's newspaper all the way through.

I recall my first, and perhaps only, real interaction with the indomitable Ramnath Goenka who owned *The Indian Express*. I was particularly incensed about the fact that the Indian government had set a new precedent by giving financial help for the movie *Gandhi* to a foreigner; what my naïve mind saw as a 'sell out' to foreign movie companies at the expense of the Indian film industry. I spent long hours chasing the story and such was the clout of the newspaper that the regular reports started to hurt both the producers of the movie and the government. I started getting telephone calls from the movie's Indian representative, a rather belligerent lady with whom I exchanged many a hot word. On one occasion she threatened to meet her 'friend,' Ramnath Goenka to which I shouted, 'do what you want.' I repeated the conversation to

Shourie who listened quietly. The next morning he entered the reporters' room, looking rather grim, and said that Goenka had summoned me and the lady was sitting with him. There was silence in the reporters' room as such a summons was rare, and usually meant the end of a reporter's journey in *The Indian Express*. Clearly Shourie thought so, as he told me to remain quiet, and let him speak for me.

We went into this tiny room where Goenka was sitting with the *Gandhi* film woman. He looked at me and said, 'you are a very mischievous lady.' Arun Shourie started speaking, but Goenka said, 'no let me talk to her.' He asked me to sit down and for a good twenty minutes regaled me with stories about my grand-uncle, Rafi Ahmad Kidwai, who he said would always steal his cigars. He clearly knew everything about my background and said that he himself was the last living 'Rafian'. Then he asked us to leave merely saying that I should get the *Gandhi* producer's viewpoint and that the lady should make herself available to me. The fuming woman walked out with us and was even more incensed when Goenka called us back to say, 'in your life you will meet many people who will drop names. If you are sure of the facts do not be afraid, just go ahead.' After that, I was floating in the high heavens, with Arun Shourie looking particularly relieved.

There was nothing in those days that made me conscious of my cultural/religious identity. I was a journalist—neither a man nor a woman, a Hindu or a Muslim, a Dalit or a Brahmin, just a communicator—there to give the facts without bias, and always, *always* keep the Constitution of India and the people of India as the yardstick for reporting. The editors at that time taught us to question governments, to be irreverent, and to delight in the power of the printed word. Those were indeed heady times, as the proprietors stayed in the back room and allowed professional journalists, and in the process good and committed editors, to run the newspapers. There were no calculations in the newsroom based on a reporter's religion or caste; everyone was a journalist as good as the other. As a result, coverage was honest, with most Delhi newspapers reporting communal violence and caste outbreaks, with a sense of responsibility and justice.

I remember being told when I went out into the field for the first time, 'do not look just for the bureaucratic compliance, but look for the political conspiracy behind the riots as well. The real story will lie there.' That stayed with me through the years, and helped me to give the correct deeper perspective to communal violence in the country. Without exception, there was a political conspiracy behind every communal riot that broke out in the northern states of India during the 1980s.

I joined *The Telegraph*, Kolkata and it was an eventful journey. M. J. Akbar, the editor, was based in Kolkata, and my real mentor in those days was the Delhi Bureau Chief, Kewal Verma, who shaped me as a political reporter. Unassuming, honest and generous, he was a pillar of support as we grappled with political news, and sought to make sense of the intricacies within. The tension of reporting would explode on occasion into temper, with Verma calling me next morning for breakfast and quietly soothing nerves frayed by the violence in Assam, Punjab, Uttar Pradesh, Kashmir, Delhi. 'I feel sorry for you all,' he would say. 'We grew up with idealism and hope for a peaceful India; you are growing up in journalism in the midst of bloody violence.' He was right—the 1980s was a turbulent decade and day merged into night as we travelled long hours to report conflict and massacres in an era where there were no mobile telephones or the internet. We spent hours in Punjab and Assam, sweet-talking teleprinter operators at the post offices so that they would ensure our stories jumped the queue. In all those days, I never heard, not even once, a comment that could remind me of the 'Mustafa' in my name. I was a journalist, a woman perhaps, but a journalist nevertheless.

Working journalists, despite their faults and shortcomings, had always been largely secular people. Caste and religion played no role inside the newsrooms as journalists shared a silent code of supporting the victims, reporting the truth, and challenging the communalists. The changes crept in with the advent of television and the rise of the Hindutva brigade, two things that happened coincidentally close together. The Babri Masjid demolition did bring about a change in perceptions and, for the first time, we realized that readers might be conscious about the byline, with a Muslim reporter being noticed, and often regaled with abuse and anger from all around. This has only strengthened with the years, as I found out in my decade-long stint in the *Asian Age*.

I joined this newspaper a few years after M. J. Akbar had started it from New Delhi. I eventually became the Resident Editor and was in charge of the reporting team—in other words, of news collection. Quite soon, I realized that, as the anti-Establishment newspaper became more and more irreverent, a Muslim Editor-in-Chief and a Muslim Resident

Editor were looked at as a suspicious team by many politicians, journalists and interestingly, even by some members of so-called civil society. The attempt to revive good old-fashioned journalism that questioned the Establishment and raised relevant pro-people issues became an issue with political leaders who used the minority card against the newspaper, and eventually convinced the proprietor to take over and toe the government line. The saddening, and I must confess angering, part was that political leaders, reluctant to take remedial measures, often dismissed a good story with what we often referred to as 'their Muslim argument.' The coverage of the controversial India-US civilian nuclear energy agreement was one such instance, where we were on the receiving end of many such innuendos. An irate government sought to dismiss the validity of the reports appearing in the *Asian Age* with this absurd argument. It was also reflected in the direct remarks of then National Security Advisor, M. K. Narayanan, to me on the sidelines of the SAARC summit at Dhaka. He was at the height of his glory in those days, and was coming out from a meeting in Dhaka with top officials of the Ministry of External Affairs. Journalists were standing around to cover the meet. Narayanan passed by, but stopped to look back and address me. 'Seema,' he said, 'you should be very worried."

Perplexed, I asked, 'and why?'

Pat came the response, 'because the Pakistani delegation was praising you.' It took me some seconds to digest the import of what he was saying, and to realize that the top security official of the Congress-led Manmohan Singh government had joined the base elements on the streets to make the usual linkage between Muslim and Pakistan, and from there perhaps even with Terrorist. I lost my temper completely. Just as he was walking away I shouted, 'Mr Narayanan!' He stopped and turned around, and I gave vent to, 'I am not here to report for you or your government, I report for the country and there is a huge difference between a government and the nation.' He left without saying a word.

∼

Narayanan was merely reinforcing the stereotype created by bureaucrats and politicians with the help of the media. After 1990, the media has gradually stopped using the words 'alleged' and 'claimed' while reporting police versions of terrorist attacks. Earlier editors encouraged reporters to pick holes in the official version, ask questions and get specific answers. Now the instructions are to go with the official story, with television anchors in particular branding individuals—often found innocent by the courts later—as terrorists. As editors, we insisted on the use of alleged, but ours was just a whisper when compared to the screaming sounds of television that tried and hung the 'terrorists' on the basis of police information that was often thrown out by the courts.

Muslims have not been treated well by the media, with the secular positions adopted by the media in the early years being replaced almost entirely by sensationalism and gross exaggeration. Sober voices are discarded, as little-known mullahs are brought on air to insist that fatwas banning women from contesting elections are valid, or other such nonsense. If there is a discussion on Gujarat chief minister Narendra Modi, inevitably the media looks for mullahs, as if to justify one kind of communalism with another. The secular voices of India have been virtually drowned in the process, as their sane views do not add to TRP ratings.

A striking example is the Salman Rushdie affair. Author of the controversial *Satanic Verses*, he created turbulence with his observations on Prophet Mohammad and his wives, and Iran's Ayatollahs put a price on his head. In India, a journalist telephoned a well-known Muslim historian, asked him about the decision to ban the book, and reported his views as if he was supporting Rushdie. In actual fact, all that he had said was that while he thought Rushdie to be an average writer, he in principal did not support bans. The news report created a storm, with the journalist's husband, a Congress member, fanning the flames. Some Muslims were soon baying for the historian's blood. He was attacked by students at one point, and sustained injuries. At the time, many stood by him and I remember huge meetings being held at my house to plan the counter-offensive. It became a fanatic versus secular Muslim issue, and with the politicians stoking the fires, it took some time to subside. The impression created at the end was that these Muslims are a bunch of extremists, with a few exceptions of course.

In January 2012 the Rushdie embers were stoked again by the same party in government. The author was to visit a literary festival being held in Rajasthan when a little-known Muslim group objected to it. The governments in both Rajasthan and New Delhi supported them. Rushdie cancelled his visit, with the official story maintaining that his life was under threat, although everyone knew that the politicians were worried about losing the Muslim vote as several states in India were going in for elections at the time. This was rich fodder for the television channels that devoted prime time to the story, with obscure maulanas battling on their side of the fence against progressive non-Muslim voices. Television anchors played the role of infuriated nationalists, with no effort being made at all to find out if this issue was really an issue and whether the Muslims in the states cared at all about Rushdie today, or were more concerned about their local problems of empowerment, food security and justice. Their responses would have punctured the calculated picture that television across the board was trying to paint, of the stereotyped Muslim dragging the country down.

The media has abdicated its role in Gujarat where only some die-hard activists are still fighting for justice for the victims of the terrible violence under then Chief Minister Narendra Modi. A television anchor is known to have gone personally to make peace with Modi, as his reporting of the violence had upset the powerful chief minister, and the channel could not afford to make such enemies. The result is that today the politician, the corporate honcho and of course the owner/editor of the media are joined together in lauding Narendra Modi, even as honest police officers and activists work overtime to get some sort of justice for the victims who still live in fear and apprehension in the state. After the actual violence that killed hundreds of Muslims subsided, the media stopped reporting the ghastly state of the survivors. And since then there seems to be an unwritten ban on reporting their suffering, a fact known to all from Gujarat but not written of.

One has to admit that this select amnesia does not just impact Muslims, but affects the poor and deprived of the nation, who too are at the receiving end. This should provide some solace to minorities, but such is their plight that it makes little sense to them when their innocent sons are caught for 'terrorism' and whisked away, with the media's anti-terror campaigns carrying their police sketches as 'most wanted' men. A story that should be mentioned here concerns a Kashmir journalist, Iftikhar Gilani, well-known in Delhi circles, who was sleeping with his family when the police barged into his house in the early hours of the morning, maintaining he was a terrorist. They started ransacking the house, seizing his laptop, which held documents that can probably be found in every working journalist's office. One of the men switched on the television and Iftikhar could not believe his ears when he saw a well-known Hindi news channel anchor standing outside his house maintaining that this 'terrible terrorist' was now absconding and the police were already on his trail. This was while the police were inside the house with Gilani. He was taken away, jailed, and, after a gruelling experience, released by the courts which found him innocent. That anchor who created a sensation with his news and condemned the journalist to what could have been death, has not apologized or even regretted his reporting.

There seems to be an unwritten code that has crept into both the electronic and print media lately: that a person is guilty until proven otherwise. This approach is deliberate and considered when it comes to minorities, as the arrest of a 'terrorist' increases ratings and circulation, which brings in advertisements. The media rarely carries subsequent stories about the release of innocents, tortured and jailed for weeks and months, the impact of the arrests on their lives, the injustice of it all. No one cares for the poor youth living in the mohallas of India's little districts; the arrest's coverage got the mileage, and that is where the matter is made to rest by the media.

A Muslim liberal gets invited on television news channels only as a weak counter to the collection of extremists and conservatives from both communities, Hindu and Muslim. The space given to the liberals is limited, as the anchors seek to 'educate' the public that the majority of Muslims are religious fundamentalists, and insist on carrying the day on all issues. This, of course, is not at all the case with even recent political history showing that fundamentalists in any community gain ground only when they get political support, and not when they are ignored and isolated.

I recall television anchors, sporting 'nationalism' on their sleeves, virtually climbing on to a hapless Muslim intellectual and demanding to know why he and others have not issued a statement to condemn a terrorist attack. The poor man's feeble plea that this has been done falls on deaf ears, as the anchors raise their voices dramatically to point out that this condemnation was the least that could be expected from Muslims. This has its impact on the viewers, who have started to believe that a statement condemning the violence from the Muslims of India alone can act as a balm to a terror attack. I have participated in many such arguments, trying to point out that the terrorists and the Indian Muslims have nothing in common, that terror has no religion, but in vain. Sadly enough, such has been the media pressure that, every now and again when the terrorists strike in India, a group of Muslims immediately come out with a statement condemning the attack, as if they are in some way responsible. I asked one of the signatories to such a statement why he felt it to be necessary and was not really surprised when he said, 'to make sure the rest of the community is safe, and does not have to bear the brunt of any untoward reaction.' But that is what the media should have been doing through informed and unbiased coverage of the incident. Instead of dousing the fires, the opinionated anchors known as journalists create undue pressures that often turn into tension on the ground.

Interestingly, every now and again a noticeable change in the 'image' of the terrorist is preceded by media reports of a briefing 'by sources'. First, according to these unnamed sources, Muslim terrorists—there never are any other kind—sported long beards, carried heavy weapons and were barbaric products of madrasas. Their stories generally centred on their religious passion, their desire to wreak revenge, their belief that terrorism would lead them to Heaven. Mass arrests usually followed, with the Indian media playing along with the police in profiling men from different parts of the country. The Indian Mujahideen (IM) and the Students Islamic Movement of India (SIMI) suddenly sprang up to justify these arrests, and the media happily and unquestioningly described the 'terrorists' arrested as being members of these organizations. Significantly, till date there is no head or tail to either of these organizations except for what the unnamed sources report from time to time.

The media spouted this view ad nauseam until, again, these unnamed sources changed the image of a terrorist to that of a young professional. Borrowing heavily from the terrorists charged with the 9/11 attack in New York, the Indian 'sources', of course a few years later, profiled the new terrorist as a jeans-and-T-shirt-clad person, educated and more sophisticated in his approach. Mass arrests again followed, with largely innocent young men being picked up in droves in different states. SIMI and IM were again the organizations given credence for training and motivating these young men, many of whom are still in jail. Those released after decades live as broken spirits, their trauma remaining largely unreported in the mainstream English media, which has not raised even a demand for compensation by the state.

Ironically, the real issues concerning Muslims have been driven out of the news pages, by the English media's laziness and incompetence in following the news. Print reporters are no longer trained to visit the spot, and take shortcuts through telephone calls and by watching the news on television. I know of many who even get their quotes off television, without bothering to approach the concerned politicians, with a certain sloth and disinterest overtaking the profession. The reasons are found in the new-found control by proprietors, many of them functioning as editors, and their inability to understand news in its entirety. The result is that while a communal riot with not very high casualties is reported as per the police briefing, reporters are no longer encouraged to visit the spot and report on the entire socio-political dynamics of the violence. In the process Justice becomes a casualty, with the absence of a media watch giving communal forces—political or administrative or both—a boost. I must point out that there are valuable exceptions, but what was the rule once is fast becoming the exception.

Money and finance drives the media, with paid news becoming the new practice in mainline newspapers. The line between advertisement and news is blurred to the point where the former are pedalled as news, with the unsuspecting public treating them as impartial facts. The media has become a commodity to be sold, and clearly what sells is not the lives of the depressed minorities and other deprived sections, but the whiz kids of politics, cinema and industry who make the news even as they break the rules. The poor have faded out of the news pages, and their protests and their lives do not get the advertisements. Hence, media houses looking to increase their TRPs and advertisement ratings do not feel the need to spend time and resources on those who cannot fetch them profits. This affects Muslims as much as the other poor, with the result that the divide between the rich and the poor, between castes and religious communities, increases with the media unable and unwilling to bridge the yawning divide.

~

Significantly, even today, I see my gender identity as being very distinct from my so-called religious identity. Or at least, as I have been trying to clarify throughout, from my religious identity as perceived by others. The only similarity between the two is that, being a Muslim, I bring a certain awareness and understanding of the community to the job—which has nothing to do with the religion per se. Being a woman, too, there is a gender sensitivity that one does not see in most male colleagues. The empathy is natural, and if recognized as such, it becomes a major asset in the profession.

As a woman who had to beg for her first job and agree to work without pay, I realized early on that the only way to success was to insist on equality, and to do everything that the men could in the profession—and often more. So, from the first day, I refused to cover the 'women's beats' of flower shows, fashion shows and other such inconsequential events. I did cover dowry deaths, domestic violence, rape and crimes against women, as did our male colleagues, some of them with the same indignation and anger. I worked late nights; I travelled alone in buses to remote places; I never asked for favours; I did more than what I was told; in short, I never said 'no' to work. The 'I' in this case is not an aberration, as most women journalists in the profession worked hard and with complete dedication. Gradually, we got rid of the stigma attached to the idea of 'woman' and earned new respect as the male-dominated world of journalism realized that women were not just as good, but often better.

Many of us faithfully followed one of the basic principles of journalism in those days, to make governments and politicians fear and respect you, and not take you as one of their own. We kept a distance, and yet developed amazing sources that kept us ahead in the business, even as we brought a certain dignity to the profession. This began to change with the advent of television, the idea that there was a 'glamorous' world of journalism peopled with pretty young things, and the subsequent exploitation at different levels that has followed.

It was partly because of this struggle to be accepted, recognized and respected as journalists that many of us had reservations about a separate Women's Press Club. I resisted becoming a member for several years, as I felt that we were not 'women journalists', but just journalists. I thought we should instead take over the Press Club, reforming it from a 'watering hole' to a thinking, happening place, instead of creating a ghetto for ourselves, away from the men. I still feel the same way, but have become a member since, because all those who had worked with and before me to create an equal world for journalism had joined with no such reservations. So now we have our own meetings and events that we manage as women journalists, and not journalists per se. The men, meanwhile, drink themselves into a sorry mess in the Press Club, happy with the cheap price of liquor and taking solace from the substandard biryani on weekends. Of course, many brave women are members of the Press Club and one is happy to note, have now started fighting and winning elections there.

So being a Muslim and a woman journalist together is mean fare. And Pataudi was not far wrong in raising his eyebrows so long ago, in a tiny coffee shop in Lucknow. 'Seema' establishing me as a woman, and 'Mustafa' identifying my religious identity, have both added to the excitement of the long journey in journalism. Instead of seeing these as impediments, I did struggle to turn them into assets. For instance, when stopped by the security men around Indira Gandhi as she walked through the dusty streets of Rae Bareilly, I used the 'Seema' to squeeze through the cordon, insisting that as men they could not touch me and should get women cops. It always worked, as there were no women cops there those days, and I could walk right beside Indira Gandhi while my male colleagues watched from a distance.

To be honest, the 'Mustafa' did not really come of use in reporting in either the early or the later years, mainly because we were taught to be true journalists, faceless and without a religion or a caste. Neither was allowed to intrude into our work space and frankly nor was it ever required. In my years of covering communal strife I do not remember being asked my name or identity by any of the communities involved. Never. They accepted us as journalists. As unbiased, secular and honest, and that used to make us so proud.

No longer. Now the people, more cynical and less trusting of the media, judge us by what we are and no longer by who we are. This is a clear reflection of how far we have fallen as journalists, as part of a media that no longer inspires confidence, only anger and often ridicule.

CHAPTER FIVE

Politics: A Trial by Fire

Politics has coursed through my blood, inherited from my mother's side of the family and honed by the years in journalism, so there was always this very vague idea that I might contest the elections one day. Perhaps. Maybe.

A mish-mash of circumstances and events led to the Janata Dal offering me a Lok Sabha ticket from Uttar Pradesh in 1991. It was not something I particularly wanted to do, but friends and family insisted that it was a great moment in history, and the chance to do something big and productive. I was then with the *Economic Times*, enjoying being in the political bureau and working under an excellent editor T. N. Ninan. My resistance proved feeble, and a meeting was set up with Janata Dal leader, Vishwanath Pratap Singh, who also seemed as reluctant to accommodate me as I was to take the plunge. He suggested that I contest the polls from Delhi, but I refused, as for me the whole idea of contesting the Parliamentary elections was to work in the rural backwaters of UP.

I was asked to locate a 'free' constituency where there was no Janata Dal claimant. By then I knew that I was hooked, too far gone, and was going to take the plunge into politics. I was also absolutely sure that a journalist could not wear two hats and be a politician as well, and so with a really heavy heart I submitted my resignation, which was accepted with shock and horror. 'Politics, are you crazy?' was the uniform response. While knowing my colleagues were right, I was too deep in to back out.

I got a call from then Janata Dal leader, Inder Kumar Gujral, telling me to pack my bags and go to Domariaganj, a remote constituency in eastern Uttar Pradesh that had been shortlisted as a choice. This was close to my mother's village of Masauli, and the connection that the Janata Dal wanted lay in the fact that my grand-uncle Rafi Ahmad Kidwai had worked there with his close friend K. D. Malviya at some point in their lives. As I quickly learnt, in politics these connections, however transient, matter. Clearly, Malviya's family had been inspired by the same considerations, as his daughter had fought the elections from the constituency earlier. I did not know a soul in the constituency. It was a classic Janata Dal constituency, with a largely Muslim and backwards caste population—or at least should have been had the party done its job of building an organization in the rural areas.

'Yours was the only name to be cleared unanimously by the election committee', Gujral said, 'so go and file your nomination papers.' This was in itself a major tick mark in my book, as the fractious Janata Dal could not agree on the candidates for days on end. I packed my bags, but just a few hours before I was to board the train I got another call asking me to wait, as Ajit Singh, the Janata Dal leader at the time, was insisting that his nominee should get the seat. The wheels that eventually destroyed the Janata Dal, reducing it to tiny parties spread over Uttar Pradesh, Bihar and Karnataka, had started turning.

To cut a long story short, Ajit Singh won the day, and his nominee got the ticket. I realized that it was all a battle for turf, and fielding an independent person from the constituency in eastern Uttar Pradesh would eat into his authority. Ajit Singh's nominee was just a dummy, in that he had no chance of winning, being totally faceless and unknown, not just in the constituency, but also in his own village. But such was the politics within the party that the election committee preferred to lose the constituency to another political party rather than allow an independent journalist to contest, and possibly win.

But I had burnt all my boats by then, having resigned from the newspaper as well, and in a fit of anger decided to go ahead and fight the polls anyhow. We arrived in Domariaganj alone and unsure. We worked around the clock and soon had an entire organization of young persons with us. The campaign was not personalized, remained highly secular, and slowly we gained popularity to the point where V. P. Singh had to withdraw his candidate midway, and come back for a second time to the constituency to support me. All was going well until the end, when Prime Minister Rajiv Gandhi was assassinated. Voting for my seat, which was to have been the very next day, was postponed. This killed our campaign as we were completely tired, had run out of money and publicity material, and frankly, had lost heart. We knew that the sympathy factor would cut into our campaign and our vote, and that is precisely what happened. The Bharatiya Janata Party won, as too many votes went to the Congress to let us win.

There is an interesting story about Rajiv Gandhi that was told to me long after his death by a senior Congress leader who had accompanied him on his Uttar Pradesh tour that year. He was scheduled to campaign for his candidate, Mohsina Kidwai, in Domariaganj and my campaign managers were a little worried about the possible impact of this on the voters. Kidwai had pulled out the plugs and for days the ground was being readied and party workers were working to ensure that thousands collected at the venue. The day of the meeting dawned, and tractors and other vehicles could be seen ferrying people to the spot. Then, suddenly, we heard that the meeting had been cancelled and Rajiv Gandhi had returned to Delhi from the neighbouring constituency of Faizabad, of which Ayodhya is a part. Our party workers were jubilant and the story ended there. Or so we thought, until long after his death when the Congress leader told me that at Faizabad Rajiv Gandhi had enquired about the next stop. He was told that the meeting was at Domariaganj and was given the list of the main candidates from the constituency. I must point out that I had, as an active journalist before joining politics, been opposing and questioning his policies. But the minute he saw my name, he decided to go back. The Congress leaders with him were aghast; they insisted that he could not do this at the last minute, the crowds had assembled, Mohsina Kidwai, a key party leader, was waiting. Rajiv Gandhi refused to heed the pleas, and insisted on returning from Faizabad. The Congress leader told me that this was purely because he wanted to give me a fighting chance. Ironically, his death took away our edge, but the story moved me tremendously.

A word here about my closest rival at the time, and an insight that gender solidarity does not really work in politics, which is a game fought with sharpened knives and candidates going for each other's jugular. It also explains why women MPs in Parliament have been unable to get the Muslim Reservations Bill passed. Mohsina Kidwai was the Congress candidate from Domariaganj. She was a major leader of the party, having held top party and ministerial positions in both Uttar Pradesh and New Delhi. She was also related to me, being from a village adjoining Masauli and was someone I had seen as a child with my grandmother. I was surprised that she was contesting from Domariaganj, as the Congress was not particularly popular in that part. But I was fairly happy as, while I knew we would be opposing each other, I figured there would be a recognition and a certain respect surrounding the campaign.

I was shocked at the reality, and actually have not overcome that reaction even now. The Congress under Mrs Kidwai launched a high personalized, virulent campaign against me. Speakers tore into my antecedents, creating a history that I did not recognize. I was described as a smuggler, a criminal who was getting petro dollars, a Hindu masquerading as a Muslim, a woman of loose morals, an out-of-work person claiming to be a journalist. One must remember that this was happening in the days before television and the internet revolution and in perhaps one of the remotest constituencies of UP—backward, badly connected, underdeveloped and very poor. I was a stranger to the area, and given the fact that we had started gaining amazing support, this was used by Mrs Kidwai to launch a false and terrible campaign against me. I

Politics: A Trial by Fire 75

could not believe it. My response—'but she is my aunt, how can she do this'—started sounding feeble and stupid even to my own ears after a while.

I realized that the only way to win an election for these professional politicians was to destroy the credibility of the rival. Given the fact that the people of Domariaganj knew only what I told them about myself, the Congress campaign managers clearly saw a weak link here and they hammered away at it.

I think what started working for me was my refusal to counter their campaign at a similar level. I gave strict instructions to the Janata Dal workers that they were to keep our campaign political, focused on the issues, and not even once lower it to the base level of flinging allegations against Mrs Kidwai. I found that the villagers started appreciating the decency of our campaign, and as the astute politician V. P. Singh told me later, it had begun to seem that we were ahead of others in the fray. I also realized that the politician has two faces. One for New Delhi, where charm and smiles mask the ruthless other face, which comes into play during an election. The latter flouts all the rules of the game and replaces kid gloves with iron knuckles. As a journalist, I had only seen the smiling face in the capital.

I stayed for five years in Domariaganj taking up the issues of police atrocities, education and health. In the process, I learnt a lot. It was an education that made me a better journalist when I eventually returned to the profession, giving me invaluable experience in the field and deep knowledge about the state and its people. Two small instances will suffice.

After the initial raw months, I turned from a novice to a pro and could tell as soon as we drove into a village whether there was a primary school or a madarasa in the Muslim areas there. The behaviour of the children as they ran out shouting and waving at the vehicle, a rarity in most parts of Domariaganj, was a clear indication of whether they were going to some sort of educational centre or whether they had been left by the state and the community to their own devices.

Secondly, poverty levels were reflected in the footwear of the villagers. If the women were wearing chappals one could be reasonably sure that the village at least had enough to eat. Otherwise, in most villages, the women and young girls walked the winters barefoot. The men and the boys were the first to be fed and clothed, the women the last.

I also was struck by the fact that one did not see old women in Domariaganj as frequent childbirth, malnutrition and disease claimed them in middle age, if not earlier. This was true across all castes and religions, but politicians and religious leaders never bothered to point out this common factor to the people, who continued to vote on the basis of religion and caste.

Politics is so completely filthy in Uttar Pradesh—and probably in all other parts of the country—that it is impossible to cut through the dirt and create an effective space for the entry of honest and enthusiastic young people. Ajit Singh brought in a candidate who was not even known in his mohalla, not to spite me, but to ensure that the constituency did not slip from his hands in eastern Uttar Pradesh. The next five years witnessed a fight between Singh and Sharad Yadav to control the faction-ridden and weak Janata Dal organization in the constituency, to the point where the feud destroyed whatever little unity that was left in the ranks. These political leaders wanted full control over their turf and were prepared to go to any length to ensure that their hold was not weakened. I remember George Fernandes, who was still a bit of a rebel then, telling me while all the others were closeted in one of their usual turf-battle meetings, 'this party is breaking down, there is nothing left here but egos.' Senior leaders sold tickets to candidates, and while the big talk was about secularism, minority rights and backward assertion, this was nowhere reflected within the Janata Dal, where the politicians ruthlessly exploited the people.

V. P. Singh was an innocent, unable to handle the party or his colleagues. He was like a messiah amongst the rural folk, particularly the Muslims, for whom he could do no wrong. The main problem is that whatever he promised was not implemented, as the ground organization was not under his control. The Congress continued its policy of patronage, hiring mullahs in every district and taking them on campaigns. Every bearded maulvi seemed to have been purchased, as we encountered jeeps carrying groups of them to denounce other candidates and support the Congress candidates, all of course in the name of Islam. Fatwas were issued by little-known men directing people to vote for the Congress candidate, although giving that party good competition on this front were the worthies of the Samajwadi Party. Interestingly, when the BJP came to power at the centre it also indulged in the same politics, with choice maulanas being ferried to New Delhi at then Prime Minister Atal Behari Vajpayee's invitation!

Two Assembly segments of the Domariaganj parliamentary constituency, Itwa and Domariaganj, had populations of more than 35 per cent Muslims, so they became the focus for all the so-called secular parties trying to win the Lok Sabha seat. Every weapon was used. Maulvis, mosques, fatwas, Islam, superstition and, of course, rumours and lies. Maulanas approached candidates for money to build mosques. They must have collected huge quantities of unaccounted funds. I refused to contribute, saying the campaign was not about religion, but about the Constitution of India. This did not work well, but since I made no exception, it was eventually accepted.

One of the most eye-opening aspects of the elections for me lay in seeing how Muslim voters differentiate strongly between the Hindu and Muslim candidates of secular parties. Not in terms of preferring Muslim candidates—in fact, quite the reverse—but in treatment that literally puts a Muslim candidate in the dock at all levels. For instance, non-Muslim candidates contesting from the Janata Dal in a neighbouring constituency, or from the Samajwadi Party in Domariaganj, got full support from the Muslims. They only wanted to see whether these good men were secular in their approach, sincerely concerned about minority rights, and honest in their claims of working for progress, development and security. Even where they had doubts about the candidate, they voted for him in the belief that the parent party could be trusted. However, when there was a Muslim candidate from either of these well-regarded parties in UP, all the critical hackles were up. *Is she really a Muslim? Does she say her prayers? Does she observe roza? Does she give zakaat? Has she contributed to the building of the mosque? Is she dressed properly?* Everything, but the relevant questions of intent, ability and honesty.

A second fact that one learnt on the ground was that the Muslim vote is the most insecure, and hence the most fickle of all votes. It cannot be purchased, except in the case of those maulvis who like their creature comforts as 'men of God'. It is not monolithic but has a mind of its own, particularly where there are political choices, as in UP. The Muslim vote is usually split between the secular parties, with the bulk favouring the party that has won their confidence over the years. Low voting amongst Muslims was rare, but is now becoming more common, especially in states where the choices are limited, and when the minorities do not see any real difference in the policies of those in the fray.

It does not follow a state-wide pattern, or for that matter a country-wide pattern, but it does tend to consolidate behind a party and a candidate in the individual parliamentary constituency. Towards the end of the first phase of my elections, old Muslim men and women would come up to me and give me their blessings, a pat on the head, an 'inshallah you will win' message. But towards the end of the second phase, in the last two days to be precise, there was this strange silence. And at the end of the day of voting, the old men and women came up to say 'next time inshallah.' That was a clear indication that the swing was against me, and they had decided to drop the outsider and vote for the more comfortable and known. It was apparent the Prime Minister's assassination had had an impact, and a sizeable percentage of the vote went to the Congress in sympathy, with the division in the Muslim vote giving the advantage to the BJP.

The last three days before polling are crucial for the Muslim voter, and hence the candidate. While it is true that all voters are affected by last-minute propaganda, it is also true that many of the castes are attached to political parties in Uttar Pradesh. The Dalits are with the BSP, the Yadavs favour the Samajwadi Party and the upper castes interestingly, have been adopting some of the fickleness of the Muslim voter in UP, but this is another story. So, a rumour about a candidate (for instance, he has a secret pact with the BJP), a wrong word or signal from the top leadership, can break a consolidating vote into fragments, with political pundits going totally wrong in their predictions. Muslim voters, like the Dalits, are very silent about their choices, listening to all through the campaign, making up their mind towards the end, and changing it again perhaps in the last three days before the polls.

A third fact is that Muslims in UP are no longer a base vote for any political party. They were a base vote for the Congress during and after Independence for more than three long decades. The Brahmin-Dalit-Muslim alliance that brought the Congress to power every time was a base vote for the party. It broke apart, and the Muslims switched allegiance after a shaky few years to V. P. Singh and his Janata Dal. Their support was unquestioning and steady until the Janata Dal split. They then turned to the Samajwadi Party, but the alliance, after being strong for a few years, broke again. And now Muslims have stopped being the base vote for political parties, but attach themselves to candidates from political parties who have a sizeable section of another vote. For instance, the Samajwadi Party remains a favourite, as Mulayam Singh Yadav has the unflinching support of the Yadavs. The Bahujan Samaj Party continues to be in the reckoning in Uttar Pradesh because of its base Dalit vote, to which the Muslims attach themselves as a winning combination. The Muslim does not like to vote for a candidate who does not have his own following, and that is one of the primary reasons that the Congress, left without a stable and strong organization, is finding it difficult to make a comeback in this large and crucial state of India.

A fourth reality is that the Muslims do not vote for the Bharatiya Janata Party. The BJP has tried to convince people through calculated propaganda that it has received a sizeable share of the Muslim vote in states like UP and even Gujarat, but this is far from the truth. There is uniform dislike and fear for the party, to the point that in areas hit or impacted by communal riots, Muslims come together to vote for the candidate best poised to defeat the BJP. Perhaps some sections of the Shia community, that too negligible, have been enticed to vote for a BJP candidate in the recent past, but this was, at best, an aberration of sorts.

Linked to this is the fifth characteristic of the Muslim vote, which is that minorities do not like to vote for Muslim parties. The Jamaat-e-Islami has been unable to make a dent in the UP vote, even after the demolition of the Babri Masjid, when minorities were at their most vulnerable in the state. Candidates it fielded or supported were rejected, with Muslims preferring secular parties. As many of them are fond of saying, the greatest Muslim leaders have been Gandhi, Jawaharlal Nehru, Indira Gandhi and V. P. Singh. The Jamaat has now floated a Welfare Party, de-linked from religious parties and even tried to adopt a left-of-centre agenda to establish itself as secular and progressive. In the 2009 general elections several

Muslim parties in Kerala, UP and Assam bit the dust, or at best got just a few seats as if they were on trial. Despite their promises and assurances, minorities preferred the mainstream secular parties. Political fatwas by imams such as from the Delhi Jama Masjid are ignored, and even ridiculed, unless these echo the sentiments and realities of the time. A fatwa asking the Muslims to vote for the Congress when they are looking at the BSP for instance is rejected immediately, and the imam pilloried in conversation and eventually through the verdict of the vote.

Significantly, the Muslim woman candidate is not an oddity. She is not pilloried for being a woman, or rejected for her gender. There is a great deal of respect, as I found in the remote villages of Domariaganj, a healthy curiosity, and a strange acceptance from men as well as women. The girls, in particular, expressed a desire to study further, but since the nearest college for women was in a neighbouring district they were not able to go for higher studies. Many wanted to work, but admitted that this would remain a dream. Not just because their families were conservative, but also because there was no vocational training or any such opportunities in the vicinity. They were somehow optimistic that I would be able to resolve this crisis. There was a general acceptance for me as a woman at all levels, but the criticism about being a Muslim did cut through the campaign. *Does she say the namaaz? We have never seen her even bowing her head? How is it that she never says inshallah?*—this, by the way, was one of the loudest criticisms that I heard constantly. I managed to override all these objections by remaining totally secular, refusing to make personal allegations or clarifications, and making it clear that my religion (or otherwise) was irrelevant in a political campaign. It did work, as just before Rajiv Gandhi's death, it had begun to seem that we would win the elections.

Muslim issues were given the usual lip service in the elections: a lot promised and nothing delivered. This was true of all parties, without exception. The Rajinder Sachar report on the economic and social status of Muslims has subsequently highlighted the discrimination, and although the report does not examine the status of Muslim women, it does manage to expose the hollowness of government policies and political promises. Unfortunately, the demand for reservation for Muslims has also gathered ground and has become a new issue for political parties to raise during elections. Several Muslim organizations have also been supporting this, even though backward Muslims are largely covered in the OBC reservation categories. As one totally opposed to religion-based reservation, I must confess to a certain confusion of mind on this issue now. Is it necessary? Will it help? Or will it divide and make matters even more difficult for the minorities in India? There is a great deal of evident hostility against the Dalits and backwards castes, with even medical mistakes in government hospitals being attributed in Delhi's elite drawing rooms to the reservation for them. *What do you expect,* say the glittering classes without even bothering to ask whether the doctor who botched up a particular surgery was a Dalit or not. The same is the argument offered whenever the talk turns to the declining standards of the civil services: *all these chaps from the backwaters are coming in, so how can standards be maintained.* This prejudice is usually greeted by nods and effusive agreement.

Of course good proposals should not be stopped just because some classes refuse to understand or accept them. But the point that needs a thorough, intellectual debate, sans emotion, is whether reservations will help the minorities or make their progress and development even more difficult. So far, the issue has been raised by the likes of Laloo Prasad Yadav to stall legislations like the Women's Reservation Bill and the Lokpal Bill against corruption (not that the last is of any real value in its present form). Conversely, Muslim maulanas and organizations have been holding meetings to discuss the reservation issue, but it has still not passed into the secular corridors for proper discussion.

One has this sneaking feeling that the leadership (too big a word really to describe the present lot)—political and Muslim—are grabbing on to the reservation issue to excuse their inability to do anything for the development of Muslims. The Muslim organizations are largely defunct groups who, like the political parties, are loud in rhetoric and completely invisible in action. Instead of working to pressure the government to implement some of the excellent recommendations made by any number of committees and commissions, they seize on one, often absurd, issue to whip up emotions. This applies to the Congress, the Laloos and such, with the BJP making life easier for them with its howls of 'appeasement!'

The need of the hour is for the Indian state to change its policies. To end the discrimination, to take action against those guilty of communal violence, to rehabilitate and apologize to the innocent arrested and kept in jail for years, and to protect its minorities, as has been so well provided for in the Constitution of India. Insecurity breeds fear, which in turn creates ghettos. Equality and Justice will lead to progress and development. This is the real fight for which reservations do not seem to be necessary. But then let there be an intellectual, secular debate and let the Muslim masses, along with the rest of the country, decide the issue for themselves.

Significantly Muslims are very sensitive to symbols. Gandhi had to change his method of discourse to become a true national leader. Similarly, today there is a wariness about the anti-corruption crusader Anna Hazare. The propaganda unleashed by some political parties that he is close to the RSS would not have had traction with Muslims had the symbols used by his platform been secular and, hence, wider in their appeal. So, while corruption is clearly as much of an issue for Muslims as it is for other religions and castes, Hazare is not acceptable as the sole crusader. Muslims, and interestingly even the Dalits, have rejected him and his campaign.

CHAPTER SIX

Nothing in Common

Jammu and Kashmir was very much part of our childhood fare. It was always in the conversation of the adults, largely because of the once close relations between Sheikh Abdullah and our grand-uncle, Rafi Ahmad Kidwai. So whenever Kashmir was in the news, the chatter around the dining room usually revolved around the developments there and, while as children, we were not particularly interested, the concern surrounding the talk stayed with us through the years. What did perk up our ears was when all the beautiful Kidwai women, younger cousins of my mother, would talk about how they would run and hide whenever Sheikh Abdullah came visiting. They would recount their experiences in graphic detail, the long and short of it being that the man had an intensely glad eye when it came to women, accompanied by groping hands.

Kashmir for me was always an integral part of India, a view reinforced by my 'nationalist' heritage. I must confess that I did not really ever question this, or even acknowledge that there could be another point of view, until I became a reporter. And even then, while recognizing that the Kashmiris had a

Nothing in Common

case, I preferred to accept the general consensus that Kashmir was a part of India, regardless of what New Delhi did or did not do. I also bought the argument that communalism would be strengthened if Jammu and Kashmir seceded, as the huge population of Indian Muslims would have to bear the brunt of this action. Implicit in this position was support for the so-called 'Indian' view that Kashmir would have to remain with India, come what may, and in case push became shove, the use of force would be justified.

My only excuse for this was that I never really gave any thought to the actual situation in Jammu and Kashmir till midway into my profession. At some point I got involved with the India-Pakistan peace process—launched, not by the government of course, but by activists. I wanted peace between the two countries, but again did not accept Pakistan's position of Kashmir being an unfinished legacy of Partition, justifying their claim on the Valley on the basis of religion.

I attended one of the sessions of a conference on India-Pakistan relations organized in Delhi by peace activists who, one must admit, had created a space for the peace constituency in both countries through diligence, commitment and sheer hard work. At this conference, nearly two decades ago, I strongly opposed a resolution on Kashmir as a separate entity, with the argument that Indian Muslims would suffer tremendously if Pakistan was allowed to stake claim on Kashmir, as secularism would be weakened in the process. I recounted the lesson from Congress history that Maharaja Hari Singh's decision to annex Kashmir, a Muslim majority state, had strengthened the struggle for a secular India, against pressure from Hindu fundamentalists who wanted the country to be declared a Hindu state. As such, any weakness about this on our part would give right-wing Hindutva forces a major boost. I spelled it all out with the enthusiasm of a Congress-influenced Indian Muslim who had not bothered to spend time and effort to understand the issue for herself. I was quite happy to parrot an argument that was full of holes, since it did not recognize the reality on the ground, or even try to deal with it.

A former minister of Pakistan came up to me, visibly incensed; wagging a finger in my face, he almost shouted, 'till when will you Indian Muslims hold the Kashmiris hostage?' I was equally angry and the exchange of words was certainly not polite. But when I recall all this now, I see that while there is still some truth in my argument about the future of the Indian Muslim being linked with that of the Kashmiri Muslim, the issue of Kashmir is not as simple as my unquestioningly conformist mind had decided it to be. I had, of course, borrowed the argument, applying it to Jammu and Kashmir without even considering the many complexities of the political situation there. But I remain certain that Pakistan has no claim on the state, as its argument is based on religion and that to my mind is no argument at all.

An early inkling that all was not as it seemed was in October 1983, when Farooq Abdullah, as the chief minister of Jammu and Kashmir, hosted an opposition conclave in Srinagar. I went to cover the event as a young reporter, and realized that the situation was far more complicated than I had believed. I also felt that Farooq Abdullah was striking the right note in those days, questioning the Congress for its discriminating policies, and yet seeking to forge new alliances with the Opposition parties in a bid to strengthen his hands in both the state and centre. But before I could really come to grips with the situation, I had to cut my visit short and rush to Punjab, which was in the grip of a pro-Khalistan movement led by Jarnail Singh Bhindranwale in those days.

As the weeks turned into months, the National Conference went the Farooq Abdullah way: that is, downhill. Political confusion took over planned strategy, as Farooq Abdullah could not make up his mind whether to sail the Kashmiri boat out of increasingly troubled waters, or make a place for himself on the national stage. He seemed to prefer the latter, and being a natural playboy with a towering personality, he warmed the cockles of Indian nationalist hearts with his 'we are with India' approach. Preoccupation with rhetoric, however, displaced action, with neglect and indifference converting Jammu and Kashmir into a battleground between militants and security forces.

Basic governance was denied to the Kashmiris, who found that even their vote was not respected by New Delhi, which never hesitated to overturn the verdict and appoint a man of their choice. The decade of militancy took a heavy toll, not only on the security forces as most of India believes, but on the poor families of Kashmir who were targeted on an hourly basis. Young and old men were picked up from their homes and whisked away, never to be seen again. Even their bodies were not found, with their wives turning into 'half widows' waiting day after day for closure. I interviewed many of them, and the stress and trauma they have gone through over these years has led to deep depression, increasing suicides and health and psychological problems. The toll has been heavy.

Today, after the stone pelting incidents in 2010, there is some realization that a generation that was born and brought up in conflict in Kashmir has come of age. It is desperate and hopeless, and wants a future. In fact, it is absolutely terrified that there will be no future, and that they will be damned to live in the same insecurity and penury as the generations before them. The anger is deep, as is the trauma, and till the time of writing this there seems to be no solution in sight, only frustration and resentment and burning anger.

However, the purpose of this chapter is not to narrate the political history of the unfortunate state, but to examine the seeming disconnect between the Kashmiri Muslim and the Muslim community in the rest of India. And to note that there has been a slight shift in the apathetic indifference of the Indian Muslim towards Kashmir, noticeable since the summer of 2010, when hundreds of Kashmiri youths pelted stones at security forces and government targets to express their anger and unhappiness with the state of affairs. The mass arrests evoked a response in mainland India, more so because of the encounters and false cases that had claimed lives and destroyed homes in different parts of the country.

In the long years after Independence, the Indian Muslim reserved his love or angst for his relatives and friends in Pakistan, ignoring Kashmir in general. Pakistan, on the other hand, was bent on fulfilling 'the legacy of Partition' by reclaiming Kashmir, and built a public opinion so strong that it justified wars and conflict between India and Pakistan, regardless of the devastation and loss of lives. After the initial couple of decades of freedom, broken only by intermittent violence, the Indian Muslim was eventually caught in the spiraling circle of communal strife that left him no time to spare for the Kashmiri, whose personal linkages with Muslims in the other states were virtually non-existent. The Indian Muslim, in fact, did not even enter the discourse except around the time of Partition, when Congress leaders like Rafi Ahmed Kidwai and Maulana Azad had taken positions aimed at keeping Jammu and Kashmir with India.

Significantly, relations between Pakistan and the Kashmiri Muslims remained exclusive of relations between Kashmiris and Muslims in the other states of India. There are far more marriages recorded, for instance, between Pakistanis and Kashmiris, and Pakistanis and other Indian Muslims, than between Kashmiri Muslims and Muslims in the rest of India. Kashmiri Pandits, however, mixed with and married in the other states of India.

Kashmiris followed their own tune and their own leaders, like Sheikh Abdhullah because of whom Maulana Azad and others were virtually denied a role in Kashmir's politics, despite their deep interest and concern. Indian Muslims barely reacted to news of human rights violations in Jammu and Kashmir, even as Kashmiris had little to say about the spate of communal incidents in North India at different points in time. The demolition of the Babri Masjid, or the massacre of thousands of Muslims in Gujarat, remained merely talking points in Kashmir to buttress anti-India propaganda. There were few protests against the violence, with the Kashmiris visibly remaining 'untouched' as one of them put it recently, by the chain of events in other states. *Now you know how bad the Indian state is*, has been the general response from Kashmir, more a we-told-you-so than empathy.

The militancy in Kashmir largely did not affect Muslims in other parts of India. The militant groups operating in Kashmir did not have any recruits from other parts of India, even at the height of the insurgency in the state. The Jammu and Kashmir Liberation Front, a violent force in Kashmir at one point in time, did not have support from Muslims in other parts of India. Nor did the Pakistan-based terror groups. Similarly, the Muslim organizations that the Indian police claims to have evidence of, such as SIMI and the faceless Indian Mujahideen, do not have Kashmiri recruits. A Muslim scholar visiting Kashmir a few years ago came back to say that this was the first Muslim majority area he had visited where his religious identity was not even commented on. He was seen as an 'Indian', part of the Indian Establishment. The distance was not bridged, despite the fact that many Kashmiris came to study at the Aligarh Muslim University, and worked as doctors, journalists and entrepreneurs in different parts of India. They took exceptional care never to cross the line of disinterest, refusing to share the concerns of the community in the other states.

Similarly, Muslims in the rest of India have never reacted to the plight of the Kashmiri Muslims by including it in their discourse. Muslim organizations such as the Jamaat-e-Islami adopted a different agenda in Kashmir, and another in the rest of India. In Kashmir, the Jamaat is closer to the Pakistan Jamaat, looking to secession as a solution. In other parts of the country, the Jamaat has never really included Kashmir in its agenda, working more on local issues of fundamentalist concern. The Jamiat Ulema-i-Hind, a Muslim organization seen as more 'nationalist' than the Jamaat, did not have a noticeable presence in Jammu and Kashmir, and has generally accepted the Indian state's position on the border state. Muslims in general seemed to share and accept the Indian establishment's refusal to acknowledge the human rights violations in Kashmir, the deaths, the disappearances and the rapes. There were no protests, no statements, not even minimal concern. Instead, as I pointed out about myself earlier, the larger view was that Kashmir had to remain an integral part of India to ensure that secularism thrived, so that the millions of other Muslims could live in relative security and peace.

Electorally, the treatment meted out to the Kashmiris was not and is not an issue in mainland India amongst Muslims. Muslim leaders and organizations have never made the killings and rape in the Valley an electoral issue. Kashmiris, too, are rarely heard linking state violence to the fact that they are Muslims. Their Kashmiri identity overshadows their Muslim identity in matters to do with the Indian state. Their argument runs into the history of annexation, and the need to be 'free' and 'independent.' They prefer to identify with the Palestinians than with Indian Muslims, as if in doing so they would have to accept a 'second-class citizen' status.

An interesting difference in perception between Muslims in other parts of India and the Kashmiris is their perception of the Indian Army. For the Kashmiris it is a brutalizing force that has destroyed their homes and livelihood, killed their men and raped their women. The Armed Forces Special Powers Act has become a major issue of contention, with even pro-Delhi chief ministers of Jammu and Kashmir adding their voice to the demand for its repeal. On a recent visit, I saw the reason for the fear, as even in 'peace time' an Army convoy moves through the state as a threatening force, living up to its image and reputation. We were stopped to allow the convoy to pass. A couple of Kashmiri media colleagues used the opportunity to climb and pluck delicious, juicy apples from the orchard adjacent to the road. When the convoy passed by, the mean-looking soldiers, with weapons in position, struck fear into a journalist from Delhi visiting Kashmir for the first time. 'Get those guys off the trees, these chaps will shoot them,' he shouted, later admitting that he had never seen the Army in this 'threatening posture' before.

For Muslims in other parts of the country, the Army is a secular force that brings them relief in times of communal strife. I have seen over and over again the welcome given to Army jawans by the victims of communal violence, when the force is called out by the government of the day to quell violence. The flag marches always come as a major relief, with the minorities lining up to embrace the soldiers as they fan out into the affected areas. It is the state police that strikes fear into the Muslim heart in the rest of India, with forces like the Police Armed Constabulary of Uttar Pradesh becoming the aggressors and directly shooting to kill the minorities at prayer gatherings and, on occasion, in their homes. In the midst of communal violence, the one demand on the lips of affected minorities has always been, 'save us, bring out the Army.'

There has been a shift, however, on both sides recently. It is a quiet shift, almost unnoticed but significant. And fortunately it has not taken a communal turn as yet. In 2010, the powerful visuals of fully armed and protected security forces firing at barefoot youth pelting stones led to this slight shift in the national mood. The violence in Gujarat, followed by the mass arrests of Muslim youth in states like Andhra Pradesh and Maharashtra, finally shook Muslims out of their apathy to notice and comment on similar treatment of Muslims in Kashmir. There was a sad underlying affinity that came to the fore in 2010 when Muslim youth were attacked, arrested and reportedly tortured. Young people bonded, to use popular parlance. I remember that after a particularly intense report for television on Kashmir at the time, I was surrounded by young people—of all religions—asking for more details, with some of them actually shedding tears in New Delhi for the Kashmiris. In twenty years of writing on Kashmir, I have never seen this in the worst of times, and the empathy indicates a change in the attitude of the younger generation.

Unfortunately, ignorance is the biggest hurdle, with very few aware of the problems being faced by Kashmiri youth on a daily basis. The avenues of communication on the internet have started closing the gap. Social networking sites are bringing the youth together, and are hence seen by the governments at both the state and centre as a major threat to continuing control and oppression. The young Kashmiri is as, if not more, vocal than his counterpart in other parts of India and shares his experiences at every opportunity.

Muslim organizations, because of pressure from within, have realized that they cannot remain silent about the plight of the youth in Kashmir and have started speaking out. Ittihadul Musalmeen's Member of Parliament from Hyderabad,

Assaduddin Owaisi, has been to Kashmir several times, and has attracted a following. The Jamaat-e-Islami, headquartered in Delhi, has also included Kashmir on its agenda, with its Peace Party holding and attending meetings on the issue. The Jamiat Ulema-i-Hind held a conference in which the issue of Kashmir was discussed, and the demand for the withdrawal of the Armed Forces Special Powers Act was raised by it for the first time in sixty-odd years.

Interestingly, both Owaisi and Jamiat's Mehmood Madani made it clear that they were not supporting the demand for an Independent Kashmir. Owaisi said in Srinagar in September 2010, when a delegation of Parliamentarians decided to call on the separatist leaders,

> 'I disagree with Geelaniji (All India Hurriyat Conference leader Syed Ali Shah Geelani) on many issues. We don't believe in his idea of azadi (independence) for Kashmir. Still, we were able to break the ice. We also feel sorry for the death of innocents.' He went on to add, 'Srinagar is a ghost town. Yeh kya kar diya hai (what have they done)? The people are very angry. It moved us to see that people were searching for milk. We were told that since the last three months children were not going to school, medicines or proper food have been in short supply. They said they were being tormented. They can't bear the torture of their youth.'

This of course might or might not be a good development. Kashmiri leaders have spent long years trying to prevent the issue from being communalized. With some exceptions, the consensus has been for a solution for Jammu and Kashmir as a whole, and not as separate religious and ethnic entities. Separatist leaders like Jammu and Kashmir Liberation Front

(JKLF)'s Yasin Malik, and All Parties Hurriyat Conference leader Mirwaiz Omar Farooq have been particularly emphatic about this. They have made it clear over and over again that they will not accept a solution based on the division of the state. Even Syed Ali Shah Geelani has repeatedly said that he would not accept any solution based on the communal division of the state.

It is a late, and as yet, a tentative awakening. But the Kashmiris are responding, and the usual cynicism which greets such interventions by 'Indian' Muslims is a little muted now. This is also because of the chaos and confusion in Pakistan, which has put itself outside the Kashmir solution, for the moment at least. The young Kashmiris are as angry today with Pakistan as they are with India, and are thus more amenable to the 'Indian' Muslims' gestures of support. Muslim leaders like Owaisi and Madani have not moved out of the 'integral part' of India argument, but they have included Kashmir on the larger Muslim agenda of their respective organizations. This could see a serious attempt to bridge the gap between Muslims per se, and in the process ensure more meaningful cooperation between those living on either side of the invisible, but still existent, barrier.

Secular parties have still to break the ice, with some recent efforts noticeable on the part of the Communist Party of India (Marxist) and the Lokjanshakti Party, along with individual politicians.

Most Muslims in Kashmir are categorical that their desire for independence does not have a religious thrust. It is a political decision, they insist, maintaining that all other religious and ethnic groups will exist in the 'Independent' Jammu and

Kashmir with equal rights and dignity. The Jamaat-e-Islami in Kashmir is today confused, not sure whether it wants secession to Pakistan, or an independent state. Such questions are answered with, 'let there be a plebiscite, let the people decide.' Further probing based on the hypothetical premise of an independent state elicits the following response: 'it will be an Islamic state, of course where everyone will live freely and as equal citizens.' Others, like JKLF's Yasin Malik who has never supported secession to Pakistan, and always supported an Independent Kashmir, are of an entirely different view. He does not want an Islamic state, but a secular state. Kashmiri Pandits want neither, as the gap is so wide now that they will not feel secure in a state away from the rest of India. Pakistan, of course, is clear that its claim on Kashmir is based on religion and remains an unfinished legacy of Partition.

It seems unlikely, despite the slight shift, that Indian Muslims will be part of the future of Kashmiri Muslims, or vice versa in the near future. As communities, both are different, and both would like to remain that way. Besides, the authoritarian state will do its utmost to prevent any affinity from developing, as it does not want the isolation of the Kashmiri to end and thereby complicate the situation in the rest of India. Even secular individuals who have been working in Kashmir to bridge the gap and address the problems of the people are facing problems, as the state has taken a decision a long while ago not to allow any leeway on Jammu and Kashmir. Given the Kashmiris' reluctance to identify with the teeming Muslim masses of India, and the latter's lack of interest in Kashmir due to their own unsurmountable problems, it is unlikely that the two will come together in any meaningful manner.

CHAPTER SEVEN

A Blow to Secular India

'Ek dhakka aur do, Babri Masjid tod do,' chanted the saffron-clad Uma Bharati, exultant at having destroyed secularism as the domes of the old mosque were torn down by the rampaging mobs, one by one. Bharati and Sadhvi Rithambaram kept up the chant, and hugged Bharatiya Janata Party leaders Murli Manohar Joshi and L. K. Advani, pushing sweets into their mouths as the ancient mosque at Ayodhya was slowly reduced to rubble.

December 6, 1992, a bitter landmark in the secular history of India. The Congress government's decision to appease Muslim fundamentalists by bringing a law to negate the Shah Bano judgment, brought it under pressure from Hindu fundamentalists to open the locks of the Babri Masjid, a dispute that had been locked away since idols were found at the site as far back as December 23, 1949. Prime Minister Rajiv Gandhi and his government virtually gifted this issue to the Bharatiya Janata Party by opening the locks of this almost forgotten site on February 1, 1986 and in the process gave a major fillip to communal forces, bringing them centre-stage in Indian political theatre.

There was no looking back as the BJP, galvanized into action by its leader L. K. Advani, launched a successful shilanyas movement with bricks carried to Ayodhya from various districts and villages of North India. The Congress government watched in silence as the mobs thronged the site, and finally the increasingly insecure Prime Minister gave up even the pretence of a fight and joined in by launching his election campaign from Uttar Pradesh with the call of 'Ram Rajya.' I remember getting phone calls from stunned members of the extended Kidwai family, all wondering what was going wrong with the Congress party that they continued to embrace. Rajiv Gandhi's clarion call gave a boost to the Ram Janambhoomi movement that soon entered its next phase of 'kar seva.'

I was immersed in politics in Domariaganj, a constituency next to Ayodhya, at the time. Advani had targeted the larger villages here and made several visits to mobilize the people for 'kar seva.' We decided to revisit at least some of the villages and hold public meetings asking the people to reject the divisiveness of BJP politics and raise their voice for secularism. Friends from New Delhi visited the remote, backward district to participate in the rural seminars that we organized. One of them was former foreign secretary Muchkund Dubey, who made a great impact. We could not, of course, visit every village, but the places that we did responded to the voice of reason and the number of kar sevaks eventually recruited from these areas was minimal. A clear indication that a strong secular counter campaign would have been able to puncture the BJP propaganda, had the Congress decided to mount one. But this did not happen, and in the absence of a counter-offensive, the kar sevaks started gathering in Ayodhya to bring down the mosque.

There was deep apprehension in the adjacent districts, but no one really believed that the mosque would be demolished, as there was still some belief in the rule of law and the secular intent of the Congress government in power at the centre.

Secularism was the casualty when the Congress Party and the BJP joined hands, the one to open the locks and tacitly support the shilanyas, the other to mobilize the people through a virulent anti-minority campaign to bring the mosque down. Secularism was the casualty when the only counter to the Hindu communalists came from Muslim fundamentalists in the form of the Babri Masjid Action committee that was formed just six days after the locks were opened. From then on, it was a downhill process, as the two groups battled it out on the streets and through the media, each trying to consolidate its own religious constituency. The argument never ventured into the realm of the Indian Constitution, with the accusations and the abuses from both sides ripping into the secular fabric of India. Macho-ism, jingoistic nationalism, threats and abuses were all on display in this communal akhara, and finally when the BJP and its supporters 'won' by demolishing the mosque, the Babri Masjid Action Committee, along with its splinter groups, went underground.

It was at this time that the ordinary Muslims found their voice, and apart from supporting the secular activists who had taken to the streets in protest, declared their resolve not to allow the members of the various Babri Masjid action committees to enter their villages. These men were not able to show their faces in Uttar Pradesh and Bihar for years after, and many of them nursing political ambitions had to give these up completely.

Congress Prime Minister P. V. Narasimha Rao, who was in the seat at the time, fiddled while the Babri Masjid was pulled down. He sat back without lifting a finger, until each dome had been demolished and a makeshift temple constructed by the mobs at the spot. It was only then that he held a Cabinet meeting, and security forces were sent to stop the temple from being constructed. India watched in stunned silence, and after the first shock was over, people poured out onto the streets in spontaneous protest. I remember that for more than two years after, hundreds of us in Delhi did little else but march on the streets in protest, hold meetings, light candles, raise slogans challenging the communal forces and pressuring the government to rebuild the mosque. That was the demand at the time of all secular groups, as we had agreed that Justice was essential to reassure the minorities that they were still secure in India.

The Indian state fought us. We were lathi-charged, drenched and hurt by water cannons, arrested, and finally targeted with specific cases that had several of us going to the lower courts for months. The entire night we would get telephone calls with screaming voices on the other side, hurling filthy abuses and threats. Family members were not spared, and I remember a veteran journalist's wife was told over and over again by anonymous callers that her husband was having an affair. Nothing was too low for these people. The phone calls to me ranged from 'get out, go to Pakistan, we will throw you there' to threats of being kidnapped. Family members were told they would never see me again. It was unnerving, but such was the passion and the anger in us, that we were back on the streets despite this pressure, optimistic that somehow we would be able to reverse the clock, and restore secularism in the country. How wrong we were, how idealistic and perhaps even stupid, as we looked on this as an isolated instance, when actually it was the beginning of a new era in the secular polity of India.

Riots broke out all over the country. Figures were never really tabulated, and the people responsible never arrested. The Indian state collapsed under the onslaught and looked the other way. The Shiv Sena, escorted by the Mumbai police, went into Muslim homes and shot individuals dead at point-blank range. This was documented in fact-finding reports at the time. The stories were horrifying. No one was taken to task and the victims were left to rehabilitate themselves. This spate of violence came to an end with a series of bomb blasts in early 1993 that brought the city to a standstill. It was said by the authorities that these blasts were the handiwork of the Muslim underworld. The fear of reprisals finally made people see sense, and stop the mindless violence.

But the cost was tremendous. This circle of violence was different from what we as reporters had covered during the early 1980s in Malliana, Meerut, Kanpur, Aligarh and other small towns of Uttar Pradesh and Bihar.

George Orwell could not predict the Indian 1984, when brutal attacks on the Sikh community turned the page in India's history of communal violence. Hundreds of Sikhs were killed, figures hovering around 2,500 and rising. As reporters covering the violence in Delhi we saw bestiality at its worst. Truck and taxi drivers were dragged out of their vehicles and set on fire, mobs broke into Sikh homes in even posh South Delhi, dragged out the residents, set fire to them and their homes, with no sign of the police and security forces. This was just after Prime Minister Indira Gandhi's assassination by her Sikh security guards (October 31, 1984). The Congress, in the process of anointing her son Rajiv Gandhi as prime minister, had decided to look the other way and for three days the violence continued unabated, with no intervention from the state. It was only after this that the Army appeared on the streets with the wailing widows and children clinging to the jawans, shocked and bereaved.

Delhi was on fire during those long days and nights. Bonfires of taxis owned by Sikhs, their houses, their shops, gurudwaras dotted the landscape. The roads were deserted, ghostly except for the fires and a few reporters who ventured out. These were not the days of television. We were accosted by lathi-wielding mobs who let us go only when they were sure we were not Sikhs or foreigners. We entered Trilokpuri (with Sultanpuri and Mangolpuri it took the brunt of the attack) and saw young men run away upon sighting our car. We saw bonfires burning in regular piles and stopped to see what had been set on fire. We could not even express our shock when we saw that the men were burning the bodies of Sikhs. We just took out our cameras and notebooks to try and count the bodies in each burning pile, to get an estimate as to how many Sikhs had been killed in that part of Delhi. Needless to say, not a single policeman was in sight; it was as if the Indian state had ceased to exist.

Rumours engulfed the city. 'Do not drink water, it is poisoned,' had people making panicky phone calls to each other. On the third morning, news filtered through, 'trains from Punjab are carrying dead bodies of Hindus; they have all been killed by the Sikhs.' I rushed to the railway station to find that the reverse was true. On the basis of this rumour, mobs had gathered on railways tracks on the outskirts of Delhi. They were stopping the trains, dragging out Sikhs, killing and burning them, and putting them back on the trains. The result was that the trains from Punjab were carrying dead bodies, but of Sikhs, not a single Hindu or, for that matter, Muslim. I spent most of the day counting the bodies and crossed the 250 figure. I went back to my newspaper and after lengthy editorial-level consultations we took the decision to identify the community in the headline, so that more were not killed on the basis of continuing rumours. It must be remembered that in those days the media did not identify religious communities while reporting communal violence, hence the quandary and the long discussion.

This was a turning point for India, even more so than the demolition of the Babri Masjid, as it demonstrated and established to India and the world that large-scale killings would not invite Justice. No one was arrested, no one tried, and for decades the widows and their children fought for Justice. They are fighting still, as those in power remain reluctant to act against their own. And what is worse it was justified by the ruling party of the time. In his speech at his first public meeting after taking over as prime minister, Rajiv Gandhi justified the mindless violence with 'jab bargad ka pedh girta hai to dharti zara si hilti hai' (when a banyan tree falls the earth is bound to shake a little). The 'bargad ka pedh' was clearly a reference to his mother. The prime minister made his debut by pointing out that the consequences of her death were but natural; that the murder of thousands of Sikhs was but to be expected. We reporters were standing just below the podium and those who had covered the violence had to be restrained from screaming out at him, the anger was so great.

The Indian state that used to respond, albeit mildly, against communal violence through the 1960s had become a partner in crime by the 1980s. The violence worked for the Congress as, in the general elections, Rajiv Gandhi won with a resounding margin and for the first time, one single party came to power with over 400 seats in Parliament. It was as if the nation had endorsed the violence, and not held the Congress accountable for the murder of thousands of Sikhs. The lesson that the Congress learnt from this, never to forget, was that communal politics could be used to consolidate the votes of the majority community. This swung the pendulum towards the right for the Congress and it has spent the ensuing years trying to repeat this performance. So much so, that it remains hesitant to take the side of secularism in any confrontation with communal forces. Be it Babri Masjid, or Gujarat.

Muslims as a community were absolutely shocked at the level of the violence in 1984. I remember the fear in Muslim homes during those days, as relatives called wondering whether the fury of the mobs would turn against them. An aunt was heard fervently thanking God that the assassins of Indira Gandhi had not been Muslims, an echo of what the minorities probably said when Gandhi was killed by Nathuram Godse. Given the surge of communal hate and violence at that time, a Muslim killer would have ensured the virtual annihilation of the community and plunged India into bloody chaos from which it would have in all probability emerged as a Hindu, and not a secular state. In 1984 too, the insecurity amongst Muslims was palpable, even though they were not in the sights of those holding the gun.

The build-up to the demolition of the mosque preyed on this insecurity. Muslims travelling in trains did so under false non-Muslim names, as they were afraid of being targeted. The situation worsened after the demolition, as minorities in India realized that they could no longer rely on the state for protection. I was returning from a visit to Uttar Pradesh and got onto a train from Lucknow without a ticket, hoping as was usual for us reporters, to convince the ticket collector to allocate a berth. I immediately ran into a high profile group who offered me space—Raghu Rai, Mohan Bawa to name a few—who were returning from a visit to Ayodha to give the artist's perception of the demolition. They were angry and incensed and we started talking about what they had seen and found. Finally a man in the opposite berth could take it no longer and sat up to shout, 'stop it, you are disturbing us.' It was fairly early in the night, so clearly this was not the reason. He then lay back with a loud 'Jai Shri Ram' the clarion call of BJP supporters those days. Mohan Bawa with his flowing beard shouted spontaneously, 'Allah o Akbar', with the rest of us shushing him, even as we choked with laughter. And then fell silent, suddenly aware of the gravity of the situation.

My father was at the time living alone in Lucknow, and the situation there was tense. Mobs would often parade through the colony he was living in, shouting communal slogans. We begged him to take down his nameplate, but being an army officer, he refused. Muslims were feeling the heat, and memories of the massacre of Sikhs in Delhi came alive as neighbours came out to assure each other of safety and security.

The demolition of the mosque had a strange kind of impact on Muslims, at least in North India. There was a never-before-seen questioning of the leadership that had sprung up in the form of action committees around the mosque. *Who are these people, they tried to get our support by encouraging confrontation, where are they now, let them come here we will show them*, were some of the reactions I recorded. The anger was palpable, as Muslims came out to virtually reject the leadership that had disappeared at the first sign of violence. As many pointed out at the time, Muslims in India have never voted for a Muslim leader. The greatest 'Muslim' leaders have been Jawaharlal Nehru, Indira Gandhi for a while, Vishwanath Pratap Singh, Mulayam Singh, Laloo Prasad Yadav, Hemwati Nandan Bahuguna. The minorities always voted for the party or the individual who they felt could provide security and, for decades, development became secondary. The demands for education and employment took second place, as Partition, the spate of communal riots post-Independence, the demolition of the Babri Masjid and other such landmark developments brought the issue of security to the forefront, eclipsing all others.

This also gave a sense of complacency to many of the parties that the minorities reposed their faith in over the

A Blow to Secular India   109

years, as their unscrupulous leaders knew that all they had to do was evoke fears of communal violence and majoritarian fundamentalism to get Muslim votes. Muslim leaders, too, thrived on this, as it helped consolidate the constituency to some extent, and give them that little moment in the limelight they were all yearning for. They were patronized by some of the political parties, brought in for talks with the government, and went around the countryside issuing threats of 'reprisals' if the Babri Masjid was destroyed. But when the 'kar sevaks' brought down the domes and ripped into the secular foundations of independent India, they were not even near the spot.

The nation went into shock, with the celebrations confined to the Hindu communal organizations of the time. But as the shock wore off, a strange and totally unexpected process of introspection was noticeable amongst the minorities. It was as if they had been woken out of deep slumber and had finally started questioning all they had either taken for granted, or simply ignored. One, the Muslim leadership and persons like the imam of the Jama Masjid were shunned, and their support base dramatically reduced. Many in Jama Masjid told me at the time that the imam should confine himself to leading prayers, and not issuing political fatwas that were bandied about in the media, provoking reactions that eventually hurt innocent Muslims. His frequent fatwas started being ignored, even by those living in the vicinity of the Jama Masjid in Delhi, and he (and later his son who succeeded him) found his influence waning.

Secondly, those who had hoped to be promulgated to national politics through the Babri Masjid committees went into hiding for a while, as the questions being asked by the

Muslims across the country, were sharp and angry. As pointed out earlier, they lost their space and gradually faded out of the limelight, unsung.

And third, and here I realize I am putting my neck on the chopping block, the demolition also broke the nexus between the two fundamentalist groupings that one had noticed while covering communal riots across Uttar Pradesh in particular, during the 1980s. Every incident of communal violence between Hindus and Muslims was preceded by days, and sometimes weeks of rumours, such as *A Muslim boy has been kidnapped and killed,* or *A Hindu girl has been raped and killed,* which would sweep through the mohallas, regardless whether it was Kanpur or Aligarh or Meerut. The atmosphere would, thus, be charged, with both communities tense and angry. The absence of the authorities left both at the mercy of the fundamentalist organizations who worked, almost in unison, to spread their version of the rumour amongst their respective religious communities. By the end of it, a tiny spark was sufficient to light a huge fire, with both sides at each others' throats to avenge illusory events that had never taken place.

In Aligarh, for instance, a row over biryani between the seller and a customer ignited a blazing communal riot, which finished the booming lock industry. Reaching there while the violence was still on, I saw both sides literally standing across invisible barriers, hostility and suspicion and fear written across their faces. 'Do not go there,' both told me separately, pointing to the other side, 'they will kill you, you will not come away alive.' Many died, many more were injured, as both communities lost sight of the fact that one part of the locks that Aligarh was so famous for was manufactured by the Hindus, and the other component by the Muslims. This particular riot broke the back of the small household entrepreneurs, with the lock business being eventually captured by bigger industry.

Till date Justice remains denied. Those responsible for the destruction of the Babri Masjid, those responsible for the killings that followed in different parts of India, remain free and happy. The victims continue to suffer in silence, carrying the anger and the scars for life.

But there was a positive development, quite by accident really. The destruction of the mosque seemed to have convinced Muslims that it was essential to avail of modern education and opportunities, and emerge from the ghettos to tackle the real world. A marked shift was the admission in Muslim circles that had remained on the fence earlier, that the Congress government's reaction to the Shah Bano judgment of the Supreme Court in 1985 set the tone and developed the atmospherics for the opening of the Babri Masjid locks by the Rajiv Gandhi government.

The importance of competitive education was felt and traditional Muslim families started sending their boys for higher education. More Muslims started sitting for the UPSC examinations and while there are no figures on this, those like Syed Hamid, now the Chancellor of Jamia Hamdard, expressed happiness that they were getting more students, and better results every year. Small Muslim entrepreneurs started sending their sons (note, not daughters yet) for MBAs and other relevant degrees to help them modernize the family businesses. This reflected a desire to move on, with the minorities clearly wanting to get out of the firing line of communalism as soon as possible. It was as if they had realized that little would be done by the state to restore Justice, and had decided to equip themselves with the tools necessary to move ahead.

But then life takes on its own dramatic colours, and the desire to move ahead was eclipsed by a violence that crushed and almost destroyed the emerging spirit.

CHAPTER EIGHT

'Speak, Your Life Is Still Yours'

A Facebook post on September 11, 2011 just after Gujarat Chief Minister Narendra Modi decided to sit on a three-day fast for 'Peace and Communal Harmony' said: 'The Ugly Indian (Modi) who has violated everything that Gandhi tried to stand for is now sitting on a fast! What a laugh, had it not been so pathetic and sinister at the same time. The fast might just about de-toxify his body, but certainly not his soul.'

This was after the Supreme Court had urged the trial courts to take up the petition of Zakia Jafri, the widow of Congress leader Ahsan Jafri who was brutally massacred along with sixty-nine others by rampaging mobs in Ahmedabad on February 28, 2002. The comments came pouring in. From Hindus and Muslims, there was no difference. 'I find it disgusting! (him fasting!)—what's he up to I wonder!' 'Pathetic...agree totally with you.' 'He has blood on his hands, can never become clean, whatever he may do or whatever he may become.' It did seem that Modi had not been forgiven by secular India, and despite endorsement by communal forces, sections of the media and of course the corporate honchos, he was still not off the hook.

Gujarat smashed into secular India. A period from which the country has still to recover as, like the 1984 violence against the Sikhs, Justice has not been dispensed. Insecurity amongst minorities reached new levels, accompanied, for perhaps the first time, by the belief, cutting across all classes, that Justice was not just delayed but altogether denied. Stories from Gujarat flew through the mohallas of India, as disbelief turned into terror, and shock became trauma. This was the first time in my life as a journalist that I chickened out, and refused to go to Gujarat to cover the carnage, more out of fear of what it would do to me and the values of secularism that I had nurtured; unsure whether I would be able to survive the evidence and stories of murder, rape and terrible, terrible violence with the steadfastness that was necessary, indeed essential in these trying times. More so, as much of my faith in the system had been shaken by the brutal communal violence of the 1980s that had engulfed Delhi, Assam and Punjab, and I was not sure if it could survive this harsh blow. I have not regretted the decision, as I believe, given my lack of courage, that my ability to be effective in dealing with the issue was sharpened by staying away.

I remember we—secular friends who were as concerned as I—were meeting at my house during those days of violence. There was a frantic call from journalist John Dayal who had gone with a group to work for communal harmony in Gujarat. He was rushing back, chased out of the state by communal goons. John was my Chief Reporter at *The Patriot*, an excellent journalist who was disillusioned sufficiently with the profession to break away and become a full-time activist working for human rights and the Christian community.

He and the others with him were completely shaken by the violence of their experience, and when they reached Delhi they just needed to join hands. They all landed up at my house and broke into tears the minute they saw us. They were nearly killed, and haltingly narrated the events to us. Suffice it to say the stories were of sheer horror and brutality, and by the end we were all crying helplessly. The violence was so marked by hate. Who and what kind of human would rip apart the stomachs of pregnant women, take out the foetus and smash it? What kind of human being would ignore the pleas, the cries, and kill with an abandon that came only from deep motivation and surety of political protection?

My journalist colleagues and activists repeatedly visited Gujarat. I, who used to rush to conflict zones and had covered almost all incidents of communal violence during my career, as well as the two wars in Beirut, did not go once. My anger had reached new levels, and sometimes sanity lies in keeping away, as I felt that I would not be able to report the massacre with sufficient impartiality. Not that there was another side to the story, but even so it seemed to me the right, and yet cowardly, thing to do. The images of Ahsan Jafri, pleading with the mob, sure that no one would kill him, a Congress leader, a secular being who had never hurt a fly, confident that he would be able to save all the residents of his residential society, being butchered alive have stayed with me. What he and his family went through when his telephone calls went unanswered, and at some point he knew it was all over. I know it was not photographed, and there are no pictures but one has seen so much of violence that the images became vivid in my mind, and remain so till today. I have not met his wife, but her face carries the trauma she has undergone, the sadness is so visible in her eyes. And she is still searching for Justice, what greater injustice can there be.

In the rest of India, communal forces were belligerent and on the ascendant. There was a particular beating of drums at night that sent shivers through Muslim localities. I remember waking up at night, engulfed in fear, and looking out of the window for signs of a gathering mob. And this was in the heart of posh South Delhi. Such was the level of insecurity, arising from the complicity of the state. I would ridicule my reaction in the mornings, until I found that several Muslim friends and relatives were going through a similar experience. One said she heard the drums beating and was sure that her house was going to be attacked. Sunlight subdued the fears, but only until the night. Solace came from secular India; individuals who gathered every evening to share their deep anger and depression. And helplessness, as the political system seemed to have crumbled under the onslaught of the Hindutva groups. It was as if the word Secular in the Indian Constitution had been erased in blood.

A helicopter-load of senior political leaders who visited Ahmedabad shortly after the violence had subsided were so terrified that they did not want to leave the guest house and came back the same evening without really meeting any of the victims. Political India disappeared from Gujarat, leaving the state to Narendra Modi and his supporters.

The trauma remained for months and years, so one can imagine what those who suffered directly at the hands of the brutal mobs underwent, and are going through. Nearly three years after the mobs had killed all Muslims they could lay their hands on in Gujarat, a movie, *Parzania*, was screened at New Delhi's official Mahadev Road auditorium for a select audience. The director was a courageous young man, Rahul Dholakia, who was inspired by the true story of a ten-year-old Parsi boy, Azhar Mody, who disappeared after the Gulbarg Society massacre in which Ahsan Jafri was also brutally murdered. The movie traced the journey of the Pithwala family as they tried to find their young son, and was a vivid, authentic, and courageous account of what happened in that state. The entire hall sobbed through the movie, which was released in Indian theatres only in 2007.

Muslims were all relocated to camps in Gujarat where the conditions were dismal to say the least. They were largely at the mercy of their God and the civil society groups who worked day and night to provide food and medicines for the people, herded like cattle into these camps. Despite this, there was a vague sense of security in the camp, so much so that when they were told to go back to their homes, many resisted because of overriding fear and the absence of security.

BBC correspondent Jill McGivering wrote the following account on May 9, 2002, two months after hundreds of Muslims had been killed in Gujarat:*

> It is now more than two months since the Indian state of Gujarat erupted in bitter religious violence. Unofficial figures say more than 2,000 people have died, the vast

---

* McGivering, Jill (2002), 'Gujarat Muslims live in terror,' published in www.bbc.co.uk on May 9, 2002, accessed on 25 March 2012. http://news.bbc.co.uk/2/hi/south_asia/1977246.stm

majority Muslims killed by Hindus who constitute more than 80% of the state's population. Independent reports accuse hard-line Hindu organizations of orchestrating the violence with the support of India's ruling Bharatiya Janata Party (BJP) government. Fresh deaths are still being reported almost every day and an estimated 150,000 Muslims are still sheltering in relief camps.

In a mosque turned relief camp in the city of Ahmedabad, 16,000 Muslims are crammed together inside the walls of the compound in fear of their lives. It is more than two months since these people were forced out of Hindu-dominated neighbourhoods—they still feel unsafe. While we were there, chaos broke out—news of shootings nearby and injured Muslims were rushed to the camp for help before being taken to hospital. Some of the injured were treated at the camp.

Nassir, whose hand was badly burnt, told us what happened. 'The mob came with police—they started setting fire to our shops and houses—when we tried to come out, the police opened fire.'

A short drive from the camp, we found the riots still raging and a group of police officers standing by watching but doing nothing to stop the violence. Just yards from where the police were standing, we passed the blood-stained bodies of two Muslims on the road—one dead, one still dying.

Officials later said the riot started when some Muslim families tried to go back to their homes from relief camps and were set upon by Hindus. Most of those sheltering in the camps fled from Hindu-dominated areas and local Hindus still seem determined to stop them returning. In other camps we met Muslims who had had the same experience. Abdul Jabar has visible head and face wounds. He says six local men beat him up—the police did nothing to stop them. "The men were shouting: 'Who do you Muslims think you are? Kill them!' There was a police post at the corner and I screamed for help. I said to to the mob, the police are right there! They said: 'We don't care—they're on our side.'"

Gujarat was not just a turning point, it was a breaking point. A break with the past, highlighting the need for introspection, reevaluation and a new path. The Muslim psyche, poor or rich, was deeply impacted across the country and a certain distance and reserve cast a cloak over their usually rough-and-ready demeanour. At the same time, one could sense a certain clinging to the secular parties, more towards the Left at this point than any other, and to secular individuals and groups in the hope that the space that had been taken away would be restored for the minorities in India. The violence fed into the 'all Muslims are terrorists' campaign that had already started after 9/11, with perfectly sober persons in Delhi talking to me of the possibility of terrorism arising from the 'Muslim camps' in Gujarat. This was a shared fear, arising of course out of clever propaganda, with the relief and rehabilitation of the blood-soaked victims becoming totally secondary to such concerns.

In Gujarat the polarization was complete. In other parts of India it had accelerated. Hindus, too, were impacted by the violence, and from initial condemnation moved into silence and from there on to support of Narendra Modi, the chief minister who presided over the violence during those days. A certain suspicion and distrust of the Muslim dominated the discourse, and even Indian Foreign Office officials briefing on

Pakistan, for instance, could not get away from the 'Muslim' view of Pakistan. Secularists came in for ridicule, with the political parties understanding the mood and generally staying away from the battlefield for weeks and months after the violence.

Apart from some chest thumping by the likes of the Rashtriya Janata Dal leader Laloo Prasad Yadav, there was little by way of a counter campaign by the so-called secular parties. In fact, Congress President Sonia Gandhi, who finally decided to visit the state long after all violence had subsided, did not visit the widow of the slain Congress leader Ahsan Jafri, following advice from her party that this could elicit an adverse reaction from the majority community! A Congress leader who had accompanied her told me later that he was completely shocked when she rejected suggestions that she visit Zakia Jafri to offer her condolences, and went with those who advised against it.

Gujarat made the minorities (all of whom are certainly not secular) and secular India realize that the yardstick and the playing field had changed. The silence of the Congress when the Babri Masjid was demolished was compounded by its inability to provide a viable alternative in Gujarat. The normally vocal Muslim community in India fell silent after Gujarat. There was this quiet sense of dismay, anger, unhappiness and yet a refusal to resign itself to a life of discrimination. There was a distance, heightened suspicion as the minorities waited for secularism to re-assert itself. They are still waiting. I confronted a Congress politician from Gujarat, a powerful man in the Delhi hierarchy of power. 'Where are you people, you have completely given up', I said.

'You do not know what we are doing, how much we are spending to counter Modi', he replied.

Perhaps, but the money has certainly not been well spent. And the Congress remains absent on the ground.

This was apparent even in September 2011, over nine years after the violence in Gujarat. Narendra Modi, who had not been happy with his pariah status, decided to make a pitch for the national stage. He decided to go on a three-day fast for Communal Harmony, to project a new image of a reasonable, sane, non-communal leader who was more than qualified to lead the Bharatiya Janata Party into the next general elections. It was a grand show, as an air-conditioned auditorium was dressed up for the big occasion. Modi arrived to garlands and for three days the auditorium was host to a galaxy of political leaders as Modi changed his headgear to suit his mood. The only time he refused was when a couple of Muslims invited by him offered him a skull cap, which he rejected for a scarf. A few Muslims with unknown credentials dotted the stage and gave little quotes to television channels hailing Modi as the next prime minister. But they failed to silence the comments that poured out into the alternative media, with the internet buzzing with secular responses to the spectacle.

On the other side, the Congress, for reasons known to itself, launched a simultaneous three-day fast in Gujarat, with its leader, Shankersinh Vaghela, in the forefront. This was a quiet affair, and the comparison would have been favourable, had the central leadership embraced the event. Instead, it seemed that the local Congress was left on its own, with not a single national leader joining in. There was not a word from the central leadership about the fast, making scribes wonder why the state party had gone through it at all. It was at best a characteristic Congress reaction: too late in the day to be effective, pointless and without direction. I wrote a column at the time saying,

> *It is this faulty thinking, the inability to embrace and strengthen secularism, that has made Modi—who before the massacre was a faltering leader facing almost certain defeat at the hustings—a figure far taller than he ever was. Secularism is an ideology that has to be pursued, nurtured and protected, it cannot be practiced by default. After all the fundamentalist forces of all religious hues work systematically to strengthen their divisive, communal ideology to a point where they can actually bring themselves to power with little to no resistance.*
>
> *The BJP, sensing victory, is ringing all the communal bells at its command. While its President Nitin Gadkari is in hospital for a stomach operation that will help him eat less, his cronies in arms are getting into the Advani versus Modi camps. Factionalism will of course be a major obstacle in what Narendra Modi hopes will be his ride to power in Delhi. Another bigger obstacle will be the reluctance of the allies, like Janata Dal (U) to support Modi for fear of losing the Muslim and secular vote entirely. If the allies ditch the BJP, then it must get a full majority of 273 seats in Parliament to bring Modi in as Prime Minister on its own steam. This is not going to happen easily, and Modi might find that the 2014 elections that he seems now to be preparing for, a major let down. His candidature, if at all, is going to unleash a storm of protest across India as fortunately secularism is not dead, and there are many who would not like the country to be led by a*

politician who has not been able to wash off the blood on his hands in a court of law.

Significantly, fears expressed at different levels in the country about radical youth from Gujarat taking law into their own hand have remained unfounded. I say this with a sense of responsibility as there is no proof, no records, no statistics, in short, no evidence that the Muslim youth has emerged radicalized from the violence. The initial radicalization that seemed to be taking place in the camps in Gujarat, according to intelligence reports and political propaganda, has given way to the overwhelming desire to live in peace. I interviewed any number of young people from Gujarat, Uttar Pradesh and Bihar and their first demand was for good education and employment. They, like the other young people of India, wanted a life, and regretted the lack of opportunities to move ahead. They all denounced terrorism, and even while some said that they had become more religious over the years, they insisted that this was part of their personal faith, and did not interfere at any level with their public life. But unlike my generation, they did complain of increasing discrimination, particularly in government jobs.

As one particularly intelligent young man from Lucknow pointed out, 'it is not a question of whether there is discrimination now or not, it is that we feel there is, and that is not a good thing for us or India.' This reminded me of those Indians who were students in London in the 1970s who felt the discrimination. As they pointed out to us, if a taxi did not stop when hailed, they were not sure whether this was because of the colour of their skin. Or if a man unnecessarily pushed against them at the tube station they were not sure whether he was being offensive. And as they admitted, it could all have been accidental, but the problem really lay in the perception and the environment that bred and fuelled such thought.

It is true that in India there are several unspoken rules against Muslims. For instance, the country's premier external intelligence agency does not recruit Muslims. A former Naval Chief was sacked as he had nominated a Muslim naval officer for deputation to the intelligence agency. He was asked to give a non-Muslim replacement, and he refused. The reasons cited for the sacking were of course different, but his insistence on not reviewing his decision was a primary reason for the government's action. Muslims are the least preferred in the military and the police forces. The long decades after Partition have never really erased the suspicion with which the Muslim is regarded in government and the elite establishment.

The Justice Rajinder Sachar report that placed the social-economic status of Muslims at par with, or below that of Dalits came as a shocker for Muslims who had never realized that they were so far out of the reckoning. There was a flurry of activity with several petitions being submitted by different Muslim organizations to the central government. Nothing has really come of the entire exercise, with the recommendations of the report never really being implemented by the Congress-led government in New Delhi.

Muslims now find it impossible to get housing in big cities like Delhi and Mumbai. In Mumbai, property agents let Muslim clients know quite openly that the housing society will not allow them entry. This has happened to corporate cousins of mine who, despite being smart, educated and earning fat salaries, could not find suitable accommodation for months because they were Muslims. In fact, a Muslim friend negotiated the purchase of an apartment in a Mumbai housing society but was told by the agent that the deal was cancelled as the other apartment owners had objected to a Muslim moving into their complex.

In Delhi, many young couples I know have had to give up the search for a rented apartment in the more cosmopolitan parts of the city and opt for what have started looking more and more like 'Muslim colonies.' In Ahmedabad, of course, the Hindu area and the Muslim area have existed in the city for quite a while.

At the same time there is a reassuring, revitalizing secular India where people accept all religions and castes as they walk along. Here discrimination does not exist, the concern is real and vocal, the embrace is warm. These thousands and millions of people do not want violence; they want all communities to live in peace, and are determined to strengthen the secular fabric of the country, convinced that this is the only way to move forward. So even after violence as traumatic as Gujarat, the victims got solace and comfort from the number of individuals and groups who rushed to the state for their relief and rehabilitation, for Justice and compensation. These individuals are still fighting the cases for the victims in the courts, and remain optimistic that the perpetrators of the crimes will be apprehended, tried and punished. Every setback is matched with new resolve to fight it through, and ensure that Justice comes to Gujarat.

There is this resilience of secular India, that impels it to rush in to close the wounds and wipe the tears. This has happened after every bout of violence, and is one of the main reasons why the hurt has not stretched into a bottomless divide, and why Indians continue to recognize themselves as one large community, regardless of governments and political shenanigans. This is also a vocal, passionate India that is not scared of speaking out.

And as the great revolutionary poet Faiz Ahmed Faiz wrote so passionately:

> *Speak your lips are free,*
> *Speak, it is your own tongue*
> *Speak, it is your own body*
> *Speak, your life is still yours.*
>
> *See how in the blacksmith's shop*
> *The flame burns wild, the iron glows red*
> *The locks open their jaws*
> *And every chain begins to break*
>
> *Speak, this brief hour is long enough*
> *Before the death of body and tongue*
> *Speak, cause the truth is not dead yet,*
> *Speak, speak, whatever you must Speak.*

CHAPTER NINE

The Flames of Two Towers

11 September 2011. 'A group of Muslim protestors set fire to an American flag outside the US embassy in London during a minute's silence to mark the moment that the first hijacked airliner hit the World Trade Center ten years ago...'

(*The Telegraph*, London)

10 September 2011. 'It was a Tuesday evening in August 2011 when a 21-year-old art student from suburban New York hailed a taxi cab on a Manhattan street, carrying a couple of notebooks, an empty bottle of scotch and a folding knife. After asking the cabbie if he was a Muslim, the student, Michael Enright, muttered "consider this a checkpoint" before slashing at the driver's neck and eventually fleeing through the car window...'

(CBS News)

10 September 2011. 'Just last month, the Associated Press reported that the New York Police Department, with the help of the CIA, has been aggressively monitoring

Muslim communities in New York and beyond, Placing clandestine officers in neighborhoods in an effort to glean intelligence and about possible security threats…'

(CBS News)

9 September 2011. 'During the last decade there have been hundreds of violent crimes committed against Muslim Americans, each with its own motivations…'

(Huffington Post)

8 September 2011. 'As the 10th anniversary of September 11 approaches, the fear that once gripped Muslims has largely dissipated, transmuting into an ever-present hum of disquiet. Molded by a decade of being watched and judged and occasionally harassed, it infuses all parts of life, from the festive to the mundane. There's the chronic worry of security at large Muslims gatherings, like the recent Eid prayer at the downtown convention center. There is the stress of finding a place to pray that won't freak out co-workers. There's arriving at the airport ridiculously early to deal with "flying while Muslim" where random checks don't feel random at all, a feeling still embedded in the minds of many Muslims, 10 years after the Twin Towers fell. "It's more of an awareness, a kind of prickliness always at the back of your neck," El Moslimany, 48, said of her safety radar…'

(Seattlepi. com)

Muslims across the world had to pay for terrorism and its leaders, created and, for a while, nurtured by the United States. It was as if a million worlds crashed along with the twin World Trade Towers in New York, although at that time no one could have predicted the consequences. The United States, under President George W. Bush, decided to teach the terrorists (read Muslims) a lesson, and in a very short period of time exported its Homeland Security to friendly nations willing to accept the processes and crack down indiscriminately on its citizens.

India, given the great 'chemistry' between President Bush and Prime Minister Manmohan Singh was at the top of the queue and decided to join the Western world in making linkages between terrorism, fundamentalism and Islam. Muslims came on to the radar and the Western preoccupation with racial profiling became a model for the government here. The first visible indication of this was when policemen started visiting the homes of not just the poor, but the well-to-do Muslims in Mumbai, and asking details about their foreign travels, and other such insulting particulars. One of those was my brother, a corporate honcho, who was travelling across the globe every other week. The cops reached his residence in posh Mumbai to question the guards about his 'movements.' They left with a directive that he 'report' to the police station with his travel documents. He had the clout to raise a stink. But soon enough, we met several other executives who had faced the same harassment and kept quiet about it, because they did not want an 'unnecessary confrontation' with the government and its agencies.

We soon realized that 'Mustafa' was not a particularly happy surname in the post-9/11 world, with different members of my family paying the price as part of international travel. A nephew was stopped from boarding a flight to the US out of Mumbai because of his religious identity. The

US embassy refused another relative a work visa, despite his having been employed by a multinational company and having spent many years studying in the US. A third nephew welcomed his American sister-in-law in Washington with the warning, 'welcome to the world of the Mustafas: frisking and body checks at all airports.'

~

The real story, of course, is reserved for the poor Muslims who bore the brunt of the US-inspired suspicions. Every big or small terror incident in India led to the mass arrests of innocent Muslim youth, in Andhra Pradesh, Maharashtra, Delhi, Rajasthan, Madhya Pradesh, Gujarat to name just a few of the more proactive states on this issue. The stories were the same, of arrests, detention, torture, and eventually, release, as none of the charges could be proved. Several of the cases have been documented in reports by civil rights organizations. For this book, I will refer to an investigation I carried out in Hyderabad, after reports that several young men had been arrested for the Mecca Masjid blasts outside the mosque. They were detained illegally by the police and tortured. The news was carried in some of the Urdu newspapers, but not a single English publication reported the story in its entirety. And, of course, the television channels did not even mention a word. Nothing prepared me for what I saw. I will reproduce some of what I wrote at the time as it reflects the plight of Muslims in India post-9/11:

It was 3 September 2007. Abdul Rahim was just finishing dinner with his family when two persons in civilian clothes came and

The Flames of Two Towers

asked him to step out. They led him to an auto, and after a short journey, pushed him into a car. Four others were there. He was blindfolded and taken to a police station.

They began interrogating him till the early hours of the morning. They wanted to know whether he had been involved in the twin blasts that had paralyzed Hyderabad. They tied his hands, made him lie down and started hitting him on the soles of his feet with a belt. The pain was excruciating. They pulled his beard repeatedly, taking out tufts of hair. They asked him to give names of those who were with him in planning the bomb blasts in Hyderabad. They spoke filth against his religion and his family. The torture that carried on for three days in his case became secondary to the humiliation.

'I thought they were going to kill me, I thought they had killed the others. I was not allowed to sleep for three days and nights. Even now when I think of it I tremble with fear, I cannot sleep,' Abdul Rahim says, as his old father, a former government employee, cries quietly beside him.

His parents cannot forget the week after. 'No one told us where he was, whether he was dead or alive, we only got to know when a journalist came and told us that our boy was in jail,' his father said. His mother remembers when she saw him, 'His face was all swollen. He could not speak. I am a heart patient, I thought I would die.'

Abdul was produced before the magistrate after three days. He was in jail for five months and ten days until he was released on bail.

His life is ruined. He was the only breadwinner of the family. He drove a rented autorickshaw. No one is willing to hire him now. He was engaged to be married, but the girl's family backed out after the arrest. There is no money to pay the rent for the tiny two-room house. They are in deep debt. There is no furniture.

There is a certain desolate look in his eyes, he is still in shock. He has to report before the courts twice a week. 'It takes the entire day, I cannot even look for work, no one will allow me two days off a week,' he says quietly.

He has not been booked in the bomb blasts case. There is no evidence.

Mohammad Shakeel is not at home. He does not want to meet us. He is too scared, under grave threat. His paralyzed father is sitting in the tenement, eyes wide, registering fear as he looks at us quietly. Shakeel's mother, Ashabi, speaks reluctantly. Two persons in civilian clothes picked up the boy. The family did not know for days where he was. Someone told them after a long time that he was in jail. He is out on bail now, without a job as no one wants to employ him. There is little food in the house for them to eat. What Ashabi did not tell us, even as tears trickled down her face, was that Shakeel was kept in police detention for twenty-one days without being produced before a magistrate. His hands were tied and he was hung from the ceiling. Heavy weights were placed on his knees, while hefty men pinned his shoulders down. He was given electric shocks on his temples, penis and chest. He fell unconscious repeatedly, but they would pull him out and after a short break resume the 'treatment' again.

He has not been booked in the bomb blasts case. There is no evidence.

Arshad Ali Khan's face has no expression. It is as if he is speaking about someone else, not about himself. But as he continues, his hands start trembling, and the horror of the days in detention is reflected in his eyes.

It was 2 September 2007. Two men banged on the door, came in and took him away. No one could protest. His father is paralyzed and a heart patient. 'Bahut ghabrahat ho rahi thi,' was the only sentence he spoke to us. Arshad's mother Mehrunisa said they had no word of their son for two weeks or more. They heard he was in jail from another family, not from the police.

Arshad says they took him to a city office blindfolded, then to what is referred to by most of the boys as a 'farmhouse' on the outskirts of Hyderabad. 'In the day they would question me; at night they would drink and start beating me on the soles of my feet. They tied my hands and hung me for two to three minutes, I almost fainted with the pain. They would give electric shocks every day on different parts of my body. I became unconscious many times, and even later there were burn marks on my chest, thighs, near the ears. I could smell burning flesh. I heard screams from other boys in the building, they kept asking me to name others, to admit that I was involved,' he says in a voice devoid of emotion, face deadpan except for the eyes. He was taken for narco tests, twice. He does not know the results, but guesses they could get no evidence from these.

He has not been booked in the bomb blasts case. There is no evidence.

Maulana Abdul Aleem Islahi is a walking tragedy. Originally from Azamgarh, Uttar Pradesh, he made Hyderabad his home decades ago. A learned man—his room is full of books—he is restrained in his dignity. There is an air of resignation around him, as he narrates the story but without a word of protest or acrimony.

It was 2004. His eldest son Mujahid had accompanied a well-known cleric of the locality—Maulana Nasiruddin who was on the watch-list of the Andhra and Gujarat police—to the police station. The Maulana was described as a bad element by the police—although the local people insist his only crime was his courage to protest against the atrocities committed by the police—and had been called to the police station. The Gujarat police was lying in wait and nabbed Nasiruddin. The young Islahi protested, and as the story in the streets of Hyderabad goes, one of the policemen took out his gun and shot the young man dead at point-blank range. The police does not deny the death, but claims that Islahi tried to take the Maulana, along with others, out of the van. This is vehemently denied by all those aware of the incident, including another eyewitness who has been targeted by the police.

On 5 March 2008, Maulana Islahi was sitting in his little room from where he could see outside. His younger and only surviving son, an engineering student, Mohtasim, was sitting with some friends outside. 'They came in a car, they just picked him up, pushed him into the car and left. I ran out but they had disappeared. In the evening we went to the police station but they gave us no information,' the Maulana said. It was several days later that they were told he was in jail by an acquaintance, but while his sisters have been to meet him, his father cannot bear it and has decided not to go. Huma, Mohtasim's sister, said she found him to be mentally distressed. He was tortured in police custody, as they repeatedly wanted him to confess to participating in the blasts. But what has become worse for a family that believed in educating their children and living a quiet and decent life, is that the police has been visiting the locality where they live and as Huma said, 'They go to the families and say that Mohtasim has named you, and now everyone is very upset with us.'

This was not so in the beginning, as the family was very popular. In fact, after news of Mohtasim's arrest broke, thirty women of the locality went to the police station to protest. They were lathi-charged, arrested and detained for an entire night before they were produced before a magistrate the next morning and released. Two babies were also kept in detention with their mothers.

To protest is a crime. Ibrahim Ali Junaid had held a press conference along with others after the Mecca Masjid blast in Hyderabad where dozens had died in the attack, and at least six to seven persons had been killed by police firing. Hundreds of Muslim youth were detained. This placed him on the police watch list, although Junaid is a student of Unani medicine with a clean record.

On 3 September 2007, he had just returned from Delhi where he had gone to attend a university seminar. He went straight to the hostel to deposit his luggage. Two men, again in civilian clothes, emerged, tied his hands and pushed him into a car. 'If you speak we will kill you,' they said as they blindfolded him. After a two-hour drive they reached a 'farmhouse' and started questioning him. He could hear the voices and screams of others. Late at night they stripped him and the torture began. 'They started hitting me with a belt...and kept asking why I had held a press conference... They made me recite the Quran as they knew I was a Hafiz, and then hit me whenever I spoke. They beat me mercilessly at regular intervals and after a day started giving me electric shocks on my ears, temples, lips, private parts. I would become unconscious...' As Junaid spoke in a monotone, his mother, sitting beside him, shuddered. His father could barely contain his anger, but admitted his complete helplessness.

The police kept telling him to accept responsibility for the bomb blasts. 'They pulled my legs wide open, placed weights on them, pressed down on my shoulders. I don't know how I survived those days,' Junaid says. In six days there was blood in his urine, he was running temperature. 'I knew if I died, they would put it down to an encounter.' He was then taken before the magistrate, and put in jail, from where he has just been released on bail after just over five months. 'One night they took us somewhere, blindfolded, and took us out and said say your prayers; we were sure we were going to be killed that night…'

He has not been booked in the bomb blasts case. There is no evidence.

Raeesuddin Khan's crime was that he was witness to the murder of Mujahid Islahi, Maulana Islahi's unfortunate son. On 31 August 2007 a large car with six persons came to his house. He was picked up, blindfolded and after about an hour's drive they reached a building. His was the same story—five days of continuous beating, electric shocks. 'I gave them names of maybe 100 persons, all I could think of to get away from the pain, but they carried on. I thought all the other boys were dead, they made me believe that. One night they took me out blindfolded, they asked me to say my prayers, I could hear shots being fired, I thought I was next…'

His mother, a widow, Zaheera Begum, said she was beside herself with worry. She had no idea where her son was. Friends informed her that he was in jail many days after he had been taken away. The hair from his beard had all been pulled out, he was passing blood in his urine, she says. He was taken for narco tests, and that has now left him with a permanent headache and allergies that are being treated. He is suffering from memory loss.

He was also taken to Delhi by the CBI. 'They were very nice, very polite, they took me there and dropped me back,' he says. He looks haunted, his eyes are full of tears, more when another person tells us that his mother keeps very unwell now, has high blood sugar. 'I am so scared,' her voice trembles, 'for both my sons. They can pick them up any day.'

He has not been booked in the bomb blasts case. There is no evidence.

Iqbal Begum runs into the room breathless. 'Where is he, have you found him?' she asks. Her eyes dull when she is told that she had been contacted for an interview, not because the contact person had found her son. She dissolves into tears, and takes out faded newspaper clippings as she tells her story. Her son Farhan had once been involved in some local dispute over a mosque. The police had picked him up and kept him in custody for three days. He could not walk after the beatings, was put in jail for fifteen days and then released on bail. A few days later, at 2 a. m. men came in civilian clothes when everyone was sleeping, and took Farhan away. He sold vegetables for a living. His father died a month after he was taken away. They have not seen the boy since.

~

There is terror in the localities targeted by the police. Sullen youth look at you and turn away. Families are reluctant to talk. After the twin blasts on 25 August 2007 the police rounded up over a hundred young men from the poor and predominantly Muslim localities of Hyderabad. A top police official admitted to 'seventy'. Many were interrogated and beaten in police custody, and released without ever being brought before a magistrate. There is no record of this number. About thirty were formally arrested by the police after illegal custody and torture, six or seven are still in jail and the others have been released on bail. They all spent over five months in prison. They remain fearful of being picked up again. 'What will we do, they might kill my boy now,' the families say as if in a chorus.

Civil rights activists in the city say that the accounts of torture under Rajashekhar Reddy's government in Andhra Pradesh rival those emerging from the prisons in Iraq. The governments at the centre and the state, despite numerous petitions and fact-finding reports, have not responded. In fact, the story itself would not have emerged from the walls of the old city had it not been for an Urdu newspaper, Daily Siasat. *The managing editor of the newspaper, Zaheeruddin Ali Khan, said that they were convinced that the accounts were completely true, and without intending it to be so, the story became a campaign that angered the administration. The Police Commissioner at the time, Balwinder Singh, later cooling his heels in Delhi after being transferred to get out of the heat, even called the editors to convince them that the police had a case, but did not succeed, as the evidence otherwise was overwhelming. The English media ignored the story.*

Civil rights activists took up the issue. Nirmala Gopalakrishnan, K. Anuradha and Mohammad Afzal formed a fact-finding committee on the arrests after the twin bomb blasts in Hyderabad on 25 August 2007. They found, and other civil rights activists in Hyderabad confirmed, that any number of petitions had been sent to the President of India, to the Governor of Andhra Pradesh, to the Chief Minister and the state Home Minister, to the National Human Rights Commission, to the state and central minority commissions and to Congress president Sonia Gandhi. The young men arrested had also sent a letter to the authorities—including the Prime Minister and Mrs Sonia Gandhi—recounting their tales of horror and seeking redressal. Every Constitutional door has been knocked at, but the state government has managed to kill the story and protect its back.

The state minority commission on its own decided to send a team to inquire into the reports. Chairperson Yusuf Qureshi appointed leading advocate L. Ravichander and forensic expert Dr M. Reddy, who visited the jail and met the young people. Mrs Gopalakrishnan and Mr Chander both said that they were absolutely horrified at what they heard and saw. The advocate said that he found that the boys were speaking the truth as he spoke to them individually and then met their families. 'The accounts were the same, and there was a ring of truth to all that they told us, they had been tortured,' he said. He saw marks on their bodies and was surprised to find that many of them had been sent for narco tests to Bangalore which he said 'were illegal as the law does not permit you to give evidence against yourself.' A top police officer of the state who was directly involved in the arrests, but did not want to be quoted, admitted that the issue was in the Supreme Court and the evidence of narco analysis was not admissible in court. He said that the tests were carried out to ascertain whether any of those arrested knew more than they had revealed.

The state minorities commission submitted a report confirming the torture. After that Mr Qureshi has been completely marginalized by the state government. His staff has been taken away, many have not received their salaries, and he is just waiting until his term expires in March next year. 'I just can't believe how well the government has covered this up and has taken no action,' Nirmala Gopalakrishnan said.

The National Minorities Commission also sent a team and interviewed the boys. The report notes the violations, but plays down the role of the Congress government.

The activists' fact-finding committee found that every law had been violated by the state government and the police. Those arrested were not permitted to inform their family of their arrest, nor did the police inform their relatives within the stipulated 24 hours. They were not produced before the court within the mandatory 24 hours of being picked up, with most reporting a delay of six to ten days. Many of those detained did not have charges booked against them, were kept in police custody and released after several days without being taken to court. Some of the detainees and suspects who have been released were reported as absconding by the police, with their families and friends pointing out that this was usually the precursor to an encounter death. Mohtasim Bilal, for instance, was reported absconding, although he was with his family. The civil rights groups then arranged for him to be present at a press conference addressed by the well-known Ram Jethmalani in the city. It was only after this that the police arrested him, with his family pointing out that this was better than finding him dead one day.

Abdul Majid and Mohammad Shakeel were picked up on 31 August and 8 September 2007 respectively. The police announced their arrest only on 29 September at Kachiguda when they were produced in court. Abdul Majid continues to be in jail, and others who met him told the fact-finding committee that he was subjected to terrible physical torture. His legs and hands were so swollen that the handcuffs could not be removed. He was vomiting blood. He was given electric shocks repeatedly, and one of the relatives of another family told us that the soles of his feet were literally hanging. He was punished for being the brother of a wanted youth, Shahid Bilal, who is reportedly absconding. Shakeel, who was also tortured extensively, is a friend of Majid.

The police official insisted that they had identified 'sleeper cells' and, as a routine, kept watch over the members. The boys who were arrested, he insisted, were members. Why were they not booked for the blasts? 'We are looking for the RDX. Three kilograms were used in the blasts, we have to find the remaining. Once we find this we can get them all,' he said. Why were they tortured? 'That is their story,' he said with not a trace of remorse. Presently most of them have been booked under charges such as conspiring in a graveyard and distributing anti-state CDs.

A civil rights activist, Latif Mohammad Khan, who has been very active in petitioning the authorities and getting the boys released on bail, has been put on the police watch list. Latif knows this, and the police officer confirmed it. 'You must have met this Latif, he is HUJI,' he said. How do you know that? 'We have the evidence,' was the expected reply. Civil rights activists recognize Latif as a conscientious man, pointing out that he has encouraged the boys to seek justice within the law—through the courts and petitions—and not outside it.

~

This was Hyderabad, but it could have been anywhere in India after a terror attack. Subsequently it was found that Hindu nationalist groups had been responsible for not just the Mecca Masjid blasts, but also several other such terror attacks across India for which Muslim youths had been arrested and tortured for days and weeks. Action was initiated and taken against some of the guilty, but there was not a word in acknowledgement for the young lives destroyed in the process. None of them received any compensation or even a promise of rehabilitation. Even at the time of writing this, there are reports of arrests of Muslims for putting up Pakistan flags, in the hope that this would incite communal violence in parts of India.

The Batla House encounter in Delhi continues to make waves in Azamgarh and Uttar Pradesh, with the secularists certain that the 'real culprits' behind the encounter that killed innocent boys in Delhi have got away. Many held for the terror blasts spent months and years in jail before they were found to be innocent. There has been no move to rehabilitate and compensate them for the wrongful confinement, torture and humiliation. This has been the story across India, as the government and the ruling establishment decided to follow in the footsteps of American Homeland Security.

Elite Muslims still have some space and a voice, and are brought out to occupy the high posts of President and Vice President. They are acceptable, but Muslims like Majid and Shakeel are not. They are scared and worried all the time as they are made to bear the brunt of the prejudice created against the Muslim stereotype. A young cousin of mine summed it up best when she said, 'every time I hear of a terror blast I just cross my fingers and pray, "Oh God don't let it be a Muslim, don't let it be a Muslim."'

CHAPTER TEN

Why Aren't Indian Muslims Terrorists?

After 9/11, the West descended on India seeking answers to the one question: why are Indian Muslims not terrorists? I attended any number of 'private' meetings organized by the embassies of the Western countries in New Delhi, over a variety of cuisines, with Muslims in India and their behaviour patterns as the sole issue for discussion. I was joining other carefully selected Muslims to help the missions and their governments understand the 'peculiar' character of Indian Muslims, which kept them away from the turbulence of Pakistan and the Middle East, and secular in their response.

Paradoxically, the official Government of India position is that Indian Muslims are not terrorists, even though covertly more and more are being arrested and detained under various terror laws.

The West tried to grapple with the perplexing issue of the Indian Muslim and terrorism, with mixed results, but in the process many of us did find some answers to the questions that were being not very delicately posed at the time. For one,

Indian Muslims are not terrorists because Muslims are not terrorists. This simplistic but real response apart, it is true that Muslims in India have never condoned terrorism, see it as cowardly and anti-Islam, and, while sharing the anger against the United States for promoting violence in this part of the world, do not see counter violence as a means to realizing any end.

There are some basic socio-political reasons for this. Not being a student of history, I am not even attempting to go back in time to understand from the different influences on India, the inter-religious marriages, the intermingling of cultures, why this is so. But it is a fact that, despite being at the receiving end of brutal communal violence, Indian Muslims have never lost faith in the democratic spirit of India. A great deal of this has to do with their involvement in the freedom struggle, their participation in the movements against imperialism, their support for the Constitution of India, which all said and done is a secular, progressive document, and their inherent faith that they can bring a change through the ballot and not the bullet.

Democracy has allowed Indian Muslims to breathe, with a participatory structure giving them a sense of belonging and a stake in the country's future. Even when the executive has been unjust, the other pillars of democracy—the legislature, the judiciary and the media—have been responsive in highlighting the concerns and problems of the minorities. Of course the weakening of these institutions over the years has strained the relationship, but even so there are still sufficient checks and balances in Indian parliamentary democracy that let the oxygen in from time to time. Like the metaphorical lungs of the rest of India, Muslims' lungs are not in the pink of health, but they, too, are adjusting to a gasping democracy.

A second reason is that imperialist powers were not able to get their claws into India after Independence, when we had the leadership and the foresight to pursue our own path. Foreign policy was intertwined with domestic policy, as India decided to march to her own tune of non-alignment and secularism. India took strong positions in favour of the Palestinian movement, linked hands with the Arab world, supported the anti-apartheid movement in South Africa and convinced the minorities that it was in alignment with the developing world and not the global powers. Despite the trauma of Partition, the country rallied behind a Constitution that promised a new, equal, just, responsive India. And it held elections while neighbouring Pakistan got caught in its own web of anger, intrigue and violence as, instead of building the nation, its leadership generated hatred against India based on a policy of 'get back Kashmir.'

Pakistan became Islamic and not secular, and this gave religious groups the opportunity to spread their wings through new-found legitimacy. Violence and terror became the weapons of the new nation, to first 'reclaim the legacy of Partition', namely Kashmir, and then to retain its influence and control over Afghanistan. In both cases, the West helped. In the first case, by looking the other way when terror groups were hitting the Indian side of Kashmir hard; and secondly, by actively arming, funding and nurturing 'mujahideen' drawn from Pakistan and the Arab world to fight the Soviet Union during its occupation of Afghanistan. So, while in the one country Muslims were living according to the overarching tenets of Gandhi's non-violence doctrine, in the other, Muslims were being grouped around a doctrine of violence that justified terror and war.

A third reason is that Indian Muslims thrive on plurality. Unity in this diversity linked them with the same issues and concerns as the rest of the people of this country. They were not all in border states where opposition often takes the form of secession. In this huge country of a billion people, even conservative Muslims can find a non-Muslim platform to support them. For instance, those concerned about the Indian government's support for Israel find themselves on the same page as any number of progressive organizations demonstrating and seminar-ing on the same issue. Those wanting to shackle women under conservative interpretations of the Sharia find considerable opposition from within the community, and support from right-wing groups of the other religions. The point is that it is impossible for the Indian Muslim to feel isolated in India on any issue. So anger rarely turns into frustration of the kind where Muslim youth is motivated to resort to terrorism.

A fourth reason is the secularizing impact of religious diversity. There is a 'live and let live' attitude that works for Hindus and Muslims in this country, and except for the odd incidents where political parties and vested interests work together for communal violence, the majority of Hindus and Muslims live with temple bells, kirtans, azaans from the mosques, and give way to each others' processions and religious beliefs. Bindis, anklets, mehndi, chadars, sufi chants blend into a harmonious whole, as both Hindus and Muslims flock to shrines such as the Ajmer Dargah. So, while there is a level of possessiveness that is exploited from time to time by communal forces, there is also this intermingling that creates a space of tolerance and goodwill. The result is that even while I feel there should be more information and less ignorance about each other's faith, beliefs and way of life, it is difficult for any right-wing group to indoctrinate more than a handful of people with hatred and an urge to kill. The intermingling comes in the way of creating unadulterated hatred of the 'kafir' as the Indian Muslim sees his fellow citizen as a God-fearing person as well, and of course, vice versa.

Besides, the Indian Muslim does not believe in suicide, let alone suicide attacks. Not a single conservative Muslim I have spoken to over the years has even vaguely condoned suicide terror attacks; in fact they have condemned this in strong words. Suicide in Islam raises the connotations of Hell, and martyrdom by suicide is seen here in India as a devilish concept.

Indian Muslims have, thus, not felt the need to take the law into their own hands. They have been trained in peace not in violence. They live in a country that, at least in the written Constitution and the rule of law, does not condone discrimination and injustice, and are part of a community that has denounced terrorism over and over again. Muslims are not an isolated monolith in India, but an interactive community that are a part of the political aspirations of India. They are not looking for a separate state as they are part of all states; they are not interested in 'liberating' Afghanistan, as they do not identify with these causes, and, while they remain concerned about the Zionist expansion of Israel and the marginalization of the Palestinians, so are so many thousands of other Indians.

But in the process there have been problems, such as the arrests of hundreds of innocent Muslims who have been jailed for years without trial for terror attacks they knew nothing of. The intelligence agencies have given birth to a term 'Indian Mujahideen' as justification for these arrests. There is a widespread belief amongst Muslims, voiced recently by well-known journalists like Saeed Naqvi, that the hydra-headed monster comprising the so-called Indian Mujahideen and supposedly related outfits, is just a creation of intelligence agencies. This is largely because there is no head or tail to these outfits that appear and disappear at the will of the intelligence agencies. There are no known leaders or cadres, just individuals who are rounded up or arrested after terrorist attacks and declared to be members of the IM by the security forces after their arrests. Muslims are of the view that organizations that seem to have the kind of reach that the IM is credited with are usually visible on the ground as well. There is information about persons associated with them in the mohallas and some understanding of their modus operandi. After all, terror groups like the Lashkar-e-Tayaba have a visible base and leadership, and even in the days of the militancy, local leaders of the Kashmiri groups were well-known, as were many of those working with them. The IM is not visible on the grapevine or, for want of another phrase, the Muslim street in India.

So, while one is not at this stage saying that the organization does not exist, I do wonder, along with other Muslims in India, whether this organization does exist. Or is it just a creation of the shadowy agencies to keep themselves on the alert, and remain involved in offensive operations to ensure that Muslims do not give birth to terrorism in India? Perhaps, and again perhaps not. But the agencies and the security forces do need to compile more data to give a body to the presently nebulous Indian Mujahideen and their supposed 'sleeper cells' that are referred to every time the Indian authorities perceive the need for a 'crackdown.'

'Are Indian Muslims scared? Is this why they are keeping away from terrorism?' This question was asked by visiting officials and diplomats of the Western world. Some might be prone to answering this with an affirmative 'yes.' But, in doing so they will fall into the trap of projecting terrorist violence as courageous, rather than the cowardly act it is. Terrorism emerges from indoctrinated fear. Fear of the unknown, fear of religion being 'swamped' by others, fear of poverty, fear of Allah, fear of isolation, fear of reprisal, fear of the 'other'—the indoctrination is an intricate web preying on the insecurities of young minds.

Yes, Indian Muslims are fearful of violence of the kind that killed thousands in Gujarat; they are scared of the mindless arrests by security forces that have destroyed lives and families; they are terrified of being pilloried and targeted. But strangely enough, Indian Muslims still retain faith in the institution of democracy, and believe that when it comes to the vote their ballot is as free as any other. And it is this democracy that makes Indian Muslims vocal, as we journalists have found in every single election, national or for the state Assemblies. They speak of their problems, their apprehensions, their anger, their resentments; they list their demands; they make their reservations about political parties and candidates clear.

And despite the stereotyping and the communal violence, Indian Muslims are not fearful of practicing their religion. They exhibit a strange confidence as they respond to the azaan on loudspeakers in mosques and line up on public roads to offer their Friday prayers despite Gujarat and all the rest of it.

But weak governments and increasingly aggressive communal forces are cutting into this confidence. It was perhaps a coincidence, but one that illustrates the points being made, that while I was writing this chapter, the morning newspapers brought home the suffering of a Muslim youth, 32 years of age in 2012, who was arrested for the serial blasts in and around Delhi in 1996-97. Like many other Muslims across the country, Mohammad Amir Khan has spent his entire young life in jail for terror attacks he knew nothing of. Despite being in solitary confinement for long periods in jail in sub-human conditions, Amir recalled the principles of non-violence espoused by Gandhi, and made it clear that he was now going to try and pick up the pieces. There was an air of resignation in his words, helplessness but yet a realization that he had to make life work for him again. As he said, he was beginning again from 'minus zero.'

It is not fear, but this resignation that is evident while interviewing the Muslim youth being released by the courts after long periods of incarceration, for terror attacks they knew nothing of. There is anger that is not pouring out, as it has been replaced by silence. At the same time, there are voluntary groups and individuals cutting across religion, who manage to make some amends. They take up individual cases, they take the matter to court, they approach the media, and they create a support system, however fragile it might be, to help the victims tide over the trauma. The state does little to help however, with no apologies for the illegal detention, no relief or rehabilitation. The youth are able to vent their anger in voting against governments and political parties, but if this trend of hounding and persecuting innocent minorities continues, it will create a situation at some point in time that becomes impossible to resolve.

Another problem is the continuing discrimination in the employment of Muslims in agencies such as the Research and Analysis Wing, and the defence services. RAW has an unwritten policy that Muslims will not be recruited, while the defence services do employ minorities, but in far fewer numbers than the required percentages.

~

The Indian state does not actively promote terrorism, like Pakistan and the foreign powers that created havoc in Afghanistan, for which the indigenous Afghans are still paying the price. But the Indian state creates conditions that have been organized into protest and violence, such as by the Maoists in large areas of states like West Bengal, Andhra Pradesh, Chhatisgarh, Jharkhand, Orissa, etc. Acute poverty, terrible neglect, and the complete absence of government has helped left-wing extremists gather support for their ideology in these backward areas in return for some levels of sustenance and security.

The Indian Muslim has chosen to side with the democratic political forces, shunning attempts by some of the more conservative and fanatical Muslim groups to organize their insecurity into levels of protest. Interestingly, even the Indian version of the Jamaat-e-Islami, far more virulent in Pakistan, has adopted a democratic hue. It seeks support through elections by backing the odd candidate in the hope that this will create Muslim confidence in it. So far, it has been unable to make a dent. In fact, so desperate did the Jamaat become that it set up a forum of secular individuals from all communities, most of them well known in their respective fields, that held meetings and conventions across the country. Muslims were attracted to these meetings because of the secular reputation of the individuals and not the Jamaat, but since the Muslim masses refused to switch loyalties from the secular to the more fundamentalist path, the Jamaat-e-Islami dropped this initiative altogether as a failed venture.

The Jamaat again sought to cash in on the popular anger amongst Muslims against the United States for unleashing a wave of terror in the Muslim world by allying itself with the Left forces. It became a participant in the nationwide campaign against the India-US civil nuclear energy agreement, joining in demonstrations and protests, often uninvited. I myself was invited several times by key Jamaat leaders to address meetings on the issue, along with nuclear scientists and Left leaders. After the initial hesitancy, we realized that the Jamaat was taking exceptional care to keep the platform secular, and while the audience consisted of its cadres, there was little said or projected that countered our secular beliefs. But this was a relationship based on mutual convenience, with both sides hostile about the other's intent, and the relationship was of a short duration, breaking down with the elections in Kerala and West Bengal in 2011. Since then, the Jamaat floated what it calls the Welfare Party. It started appearing at progressive demonstrations to gain some levels of credibility. It did field a few candidates in Uttar Pradesh during the Assembly elections in 2012, seeking an alliance with the secular parties, but was not seen as viable and was rejected by the political parties as well as the Muslim masses.

Muslims in India do not like religious outfits adopting political hues. The two are seen as separate here, even though the conservatives claim that in Islam religion and politics are inseparable. But the Indian Muslim has decided to keep the two separate, and does not take kindly to attempts to influence the political vote with a purely religious argument.

I remember my first visit to Deoband, the school of Islamic thought, as a cub reporter. I was surprised to find scores of young, intelligent young boys receiving an education that did not prepare them for the modern world, only for seminaries. Some with a little more ambition told me they would look for jobs as interpreters for Arabic, and perhaps a handful did succeed. I spoke to the head of the institution at the time—this was in the early 1980s—and found him to be far removed from the times although, of course, he was clearly a good, decent gentleman. He got irritated with my line of questioning which wondered how religious education could answer the problem of unemployment for the Muslim youth today. And why Deoband insisted on giving fatwas that served to establish Islam as a regressive and not a progressive religion. Is there not a need to re-interpret the rather open-ended verses of the Quran, I asked. I did not get any answers, just a sermon about my ignorance.

Interestingly, despite their respect for Deoband and its scholars, Muslims have chosen to ignore the various fatwas that have a political flavour. Muslim women, for instance, have given short shift to a fatwa questioning their right to contest elections, with a group of young women shrugging off my questions on this with a 'well, we don't think these are binding.' Similarly the imams of Delhi's Jama Masjid, both the father and now the son, have lost credibility because of their political fatwas directing the Muslims to vote for one or the other party. The Muslims living in and around Jama Masjid make it clear that the imam is there to lead the prayers, and not to tell them who to vote for. To the last person, from the shopkeeper to the rickshaw puller, to the small-time politician, the response was the same, 'we will vote who we want to vote for, this is not the imam's business.' The politicians have finally realized this, and the imam is not as actively sought after as he was by political parties seeking a fatwa in their favour. It is a similar case with most clerics in the states now, with Muslim voters openly ridiculing the 'mullahs for sale' and the politicians who line up to purchase them. In Uttar Pradesh, where the Muslim vote is at its most influential, they have repeatedly rejected local and so-called 'national' fatwas and voted for the political party they feel most suited to fulfill their demands and needs.

The religious influence thus, is weak on the Indian Muslims when they exercise their political rights. They do not vote for the protection of their religion, as that is already guaranteed under the Constitution of India. And in their long experience, the law works better than the clerics in this aspect. Terrorism and violence as a means to any end is not in their blood, as they are part of India where this has not taken hold.

Just for the record, it is interesting to note that in 2005, at the end of the long weeks of discussions with Muslims, the United States Ambassador to India, David Mulford, sent a few cables to the US State Department, which were released by Wikileaks recently. One of these said:

> India's over 150 million Muslim population is largely un-attracted to extremism. Separatism and religious extremism have little appeal to Indian Muslims, and the overwhelming majority espouse moderate doctrine.
>
> With Indian Muslim youth increasingly comfortable in the mainstream, the pool of potential recruits is shrinking, while Muslim families and communities provide little sanction or support to extremist appeals.
>
> Islamic extremism is not popular in India and most adults are not interested. This forces extremists to pitch to young and naïve audiences who may be more amenable.

And again in another cable:

> India's Muslim population is estimated to be as large as 150 million (the second-largest in the world after Indonesia), and suffers from higher rates of poverty than most other groups in India, and can be the victims of discrimination and prejudice. Despite this, the vast majority remain committed to the Indian state and seek to participate in mainstream political and economic life.

There were widespread anger and demonstrations in Delhi over the sudden arrest of a well-known Urdu journalist, Syed Mohammed Ahmad Kazmi, for alleged involvement in an attack on an Israeli diplomat in February 2012. After denying Israeli claims that the attack, in which the diplomat was mildly hurt, was planned and executed by Iran, the UPA government in Delhi took an about-turn and arrested Kazmi who was working with the Iranian news agency. Such was the level of disbelief that journalists and activists immediately came out on to the streets in protest, maintaining that the government was buckling under the combined pressure of the US and Israel. Journalists who held several meetings on the issue pointed out that Kazmi was a regular visitor to West Asia and his reports had contradicted much of the propaganda of the US and Israel on the situation in Iran and other countries in the region.

There was some disquiet amongst the secular ranks when the Jama Masjid Imam, Syed Ahmed Bukhari, joined Kazmi's family in support, and organized his followers into a fairly vociferous protest against his arrest. However, many took it in their stride, pointing out that there was sufficient room for everyone on this issue. And as a senior journalist pointed out, 'it is good to see a Sunni cleric protesting against the arrest of a Shia journalist.' Kazmi, at the time of writing this, continues to be in prison, with no word from the authorities about the charges against him, or his possible release on bail.

CHAPTER ELEVEN

The Night Before a Dawn

Mumbai was in the grip of terror in 2008. All of Indian mourned the terrible attack by Pakistani terrorist, Mohammed Ajmal Amir Kasab, and his compatriots in arms, in which dozens of Indians, both Hindus and Muslims, were mowed down on the streets and inside buildings, including in a five-star hotel. A strong wave of sorrow that quickly turned into deep anger rumbled through the nation, as all united to condemn the violence and demand international action against Pakistan for planning and executing the attack. Muslim organizations rushed out to issue statements against the attack as the country united behind the dead.

My cousin's husband, Hasan Ghafoor, was the Police Commissioner of Mumbai at the time. An honest, decent and competent soul, he worked around the clock to keep the city safe. Even so, he eventually fell prey to the politics that had touched another amazingly honest and courageous police officer, Hemant Karkare, who, as the chief of the Mumbai Anti Terrorist Squad (ATS), had created waves by defying the common wisdom created by the right-wing political parties and the media, and arresting radical Hindus and not Muslims for terror attacks in the city in 2008. Karkare came under tremendous pressure from political parties like the Shiv Sena, the Bharatiya Janata Party and outfits like the vitriolic Vishwa Hindu Parishad but, armed with evidence, he stood his ground. He was killed in circumstances described by many as 'mysterious' when he accompanied his colleagues to counter the terrorists who devastated Mumbai. A television news channel later ran an expose alleging that Karkare was given a sub-standard bulletproof jacket, but this was never proved as the jacket conveniently disappeared from the hospital where he was taken after sustaining three bullets in his chest.

Ghafoor died a natural death, but the attack launched against him by avaricious police officers looking for promotions and postings in his stead disturbed him deeply. These men and their political mentors ran a virtual campaign against the police officer lauded by the Mumbai citizen for his honesty and integrity, with stories being planted in the media against him on a fairly regular basis. Not a person to speak out, he internalized the stress and died suddenly, leaving his wife and daughter traumatized. It almost seemed as if there was no space for truly secular police officers in Mumbai, men who were doing their job without fear or favour.

As 24-hour television moved into Mumbai to cover the terror attack, all ethics and responsibility vanished into the air. Commando operations designed to take the terrorists, who were holed up in a Jewish household, by surprise were caught on camera and televised for the entire world to see and for the terrorists to be warned. Given television's preoccupation with TRP ratings, the coverage remained almost exclusively focused on the deaths and destruction in the luxury hotel, with the main carnage on the streets passing muster. Chat shows at night followed the day-long coverage, as the terrible news turned into dark entertainment for the star anchors beating their breasts as if they, and not the people of Mumbai, were the victims. The guests were mostly celebrities, as they 'sell' more than the poor, who just have to live with what they suffer. Perhaps the lasting image was of celebrity and former actor Simi Garewal, looking as always impeccable in white. She recounted her horror at looking down from obviously a high-rise building on to the slums below to see these 'Pakistani' flags on the jhuggi tops. She made it sound as if Muslims were celebrating the terror attack with Pakistan's flags waving in the breeze. This could have been a factor to incite violence, but fortunately her words sounded too stupid for communal bigots to get excited about. She attracted considerable flak from secularists across the country, but the damage in one sense was done, and the Indian Muslim equated once again at a particularly sensitive juncture with Pakistan and terrorism, on national television.

This tendency to club Muslims into a monolith, as if there are no individual or cultural or gender differences, has created resentment within sections of the community for years now. Many who had accepted it unquestioningly in the past are raising serious questions now about this tendency to look on the minorities as one unit with one reaction, and of course, one vote. The Muslim in Kerala has culturally more in common with the Hindu in his state than the biryani-eating Muslim of Awadh. They eat different foods, they speak a different language, and often find that religious identity is not sufficient to bind them together in one orthodox grouping.

~

There are some issues however, that have affected the community at large and elicited fairly similar reactions across the board. The demolition of the Babri Masjid reverberated in the south as well, with Muslims across India responding to the communalization and the sheer injustice of the act. But here the reaction was part of a larger secular response that consolidated to fight back against what was widely perceived as a Hindutva onslaught. Muslims, even the more conservative amongst them, joined the secular offensive and participated in all-night vigils, candlelight processions and demonstrations against the attack on the Constitution of India as explained earlier in this book.

Another major issue that had a national impact was the massacre of Muslims in Gujarat. Here there were some unsuccessful attempts to polarize victims of the violence on communal lines, but these were overtaken by the larger secular response. The result was that even the victims of the violence sought refuge in the courts of law, and fought the communalists with the Constitution and the rule of law. This, despite murmurs heard in the security establishment of Muslims becoming terrorists, which led to large scale arrests in various parts of the country, but did not take away from the fact that the minorities were looking at secular and not communal or, for that matter, terror responses to the pogrom.

Unfortunately, this wisdom gets eclipsed when it comes to what the minorities perceive as an attack on their religious beliefs. A case in point is the Shah Bano judgment, discussed earlier in this book, where the patriarchal Muslims came together to oppose maintenance rights for divorced Muslim women. They justified their opposition with the argument that the courts had no right to intervene in Muslim Law, and that this would spell the end of independent Islamic jurisprudence and the freedom to follow the religious tenets of Islam. Here there was a sharp division between the liberals and the conservatives, with the former more concerned about the rights of Muslim women and the need for reform within Personal Law, while the latter raised the bogey of 'Islam in danger' to have their way with the government of the day.

An issue with a pan-Muslim appeal concerns author Salman Rushdie and his book *Satanic Verses*. A practicing Muslim, conservative or liberal, will find it almost impossible to condone what the author has written, although many in India have publicly taken a principled position against a ban on books, art and cinema. Initially there was widespread reaction, with the community virtually acting as one against the perceived attack on Prophet Mohammad and his family. At the same time, after the initial fervour of the Ayatollahs, Muslims in India dropped this as an issue of any consequence and actually have no problem with Rushdie walking in and out of the country so long as he leaves Islam and their religious beliefs alone. At the Jaipur Literary Festival in January 2012, a group of mullahs had little to no support outside when they demanded a ban on the entry of Rushdie, but unfortunately exaggerated media coverage gave them a handle for their own publicity. In the process, the Muslims-versus-Progress stereotyping got a major boost, with the media not even bothering to point out that these mullahs did not represent the community at any level. Or that Muslims were certainly not a monolith, scrambling to save their faith at the cost of development and progress.

Darul Uloom Deoband has from time to time got on to the media scanner, and its fatwas in particular excite quite a reaction. These have more impact on the non-Muslims and the media in terms of reactions, than on the poor Muslim who has little time for these niceties of law. Take the fatwa issued by Deoband declaring that Muslims should not celebrate birthdays. This was countered by the Sufi strand of thought, the All India Ulema and Mashaikh Board which accused Deoband of propagating hard Wahabism, and pointed out that there was no such ban on the celebration of birthdays in Islam. The fatwa has had no impact on Muslims who continue with life as before. This has been the fate of most such fatwas, as life is tough enough for the minorities and the poor without the additional pressure of such decrees.

Another fatwa by the seminary directing Muslim women not to work drew tremendous flak from the community, as well as from other Muslim clerics. 'It is unlawful (under Sharia law) for Muslim women to work in the government or private sector where men and women work together and women have to talk with men frankly and without a veil,' the fatwa stated. But in an environment where employment is valued for both men and women, this was immediately countered by Muslims, and despite remaining in the public domain has clearly not had an impact on the community.

~

An issue that is being raised by political parties in a bid to get the Muslim vote is that of reservations for the community. Muslim organizations, after the publication of the Justice Rajinder Sachar Report on the Economic and Social status of Muslims in India, held several meetings to highlight this one demand. This was really in response to the shock that greeted the report's observations placing Muslims at par with, or even below, Dalits on the socio-economic front. The indicators taken by the report to evaluate the status of Muslims read very poorly for the community, and acted as a nasty jab, awakening the masses to their plight in independent India. A question that was asked in almost every Muslim household at the time was, 'how and when did this happen? Now what is going to be done about it?'

Muslim organizations who have done little for the development of the community held meetings to deflect the pressure, and demanded reservations in jobs. Before the Assembly elections in Uttar Pradesh and with an eye on the crucial Muslim vote, the Congress came on to the bandwagon that had been hitherto occupied by the Samajwadi Party and the Bahujan Samaj Party only. Interestingly though, the issue of reservations was not echoed in UP towns where ordinary Muslims interviewed randomly by me during an election tour spoke of the need for equal opportunities, employment generation and development. Reservation, they said, was fine so long as it ensured employment but most were cynical of the outcome. Interestingly, backward Muslims who have been included in the Mandal Commission reservation for Other Backward Castes were not particularly in favour of reservation for the community, maintaining that there was the danger of the not-so-backward Muslims grabbing the spoils of reservation.

The Mandal Commission was instituted in 1979 by the Janata Party government under Prime Minister Morarji Desai to 'identify the socially or educationally backward' classes and to study their status. It was headed by an Indian parliamentarian, Bindeshwari Prasad Mandal, and recommended affirmative action for the Other Backward Classes along with the Scheduled Castes and Tribes. The Commission was not in favour of reservation for Muslims as a religious community. It instead addressed the problem of backwardness amongst the minorities by identifying and including at least eighty Muslim groups for reservations. There is no study to determine whether these Muslim groups have benefited from it, but then the larger impact of the Mandal Commission in ensuring the socio-economic progress of the OBCs still remains a matter of speculation in the absence of concrete statistics and data. To my mind, proper implementation of the provisions for backward Muslim groups would help in the uplift of the community as a whole and there is no need for further reservation based on religion.

Again, it is clear that the Muslim masses are not reacting as a monolith, although the political parties and the Muslim elite seem to have picked on reservations as a panacea for the lack of growth and development within the community. I myself am still not sure about religion-based reservation, as this could widen the divide and create more problems for Muslims. Also, Muslims do not suffer from a caste system, making sections untouchable and unacceptable. There is discrimination as a whole, but that could increase, and not lessen, with reservation.

There is of course a need for urgent measures to bring the community at par with the rest of the country on the socio-economic scale, but this can be done through an aggressive implementation of existing recommendations, as given by the Sachar and a host of other reports that cover education, vocational training, recruitment, employment and job opportunities for the minority community. Unfortunately, instead of doing this in a determined manner, governments of the day are spending time beating the drums over the issue of reservation, which has already elicited hostile and divisive reactions from the BJP and the Hindutva brigade. This, of course, is not a reason for scuttling the demand, but it is important for the political parties and Muslim organizations to honestly assess whether the advantages of reservation will outweigh the disadvantages in the long term. In their hurry to rule, Jawaharlal Nehru and Mohammad Ali Jinnah did not make such an assessment about Partition, and Muslim decline can be linked directly to the failure of post-Independence governments to erase the inequalities and the injustice of this religion-based division of the country. Reservation could be the new diversionary, and perhaps disastrous, mantra by the political class, and hence needs to be studied and understood in all its dimensions.

Development and progress is a big issue now for Muslims, who do not want their own, and the government's attention to be diverted from it. In every election, especially in Uttar Pradesh or Bihar, which are recognized as the two most backward states of India, Muslims have joined the rest in demanding education and employment opportunities. There is a growing realization that these are the weapons of modern India and evident desire to acquire them. It is an issue that the political parties will have to grapple with in the days to come, as the Muslim vote bank is very clearly looking for the candidate and the party who can deliver on the economic front.

One important aspect of this is the very low percentage of Muslims in government jobs. The documented evidence now available proves that Muslims lag behind all other groups in the education and job sector. For instance, the representation of Muslims in the central government services has gone down, and not increased. It was 2.98 per cent in 1981 and 2.3 per cent in 2000. This, of course, makes a case for the pro-reservation groups who point out that a reservation percentage could only improve, and not worsen, this picture. There is an overriding concern, rapidly turning into a fear, of being left out. Of being destined to sit on the sidelines, impoverished and insecure.

This is one of the main reasons why Muslims, even in the North Indian states, have discarded Babri Masjid as an issue. Regardless of the fact that Justice has not followed the demolition, the Muslim masses are clear that they do not want to dwell in the past, as it could weigh them down indefinitely. They want to shed the baggage and move on. Secular groups observing the anniversary of the demolition on every December 6 as part of principled politics seeking accountability find fewer and fewer Muslims willing to join them on this issue. On the other hand, meetings centred around employment

The Night Before a Dawn

opportunities draw in the young and earnest, who are looking for a more equal and prosperous future.

Security remains an overriding issue, however. Communal violence has dotted the Indian landscape since Independence and made minorities fearful and particularly concerned about their security. In Uttar Pradesh we have reported on elections following communal violence as well as those held in a more level playing field. To give two examples: in the polls after the Babri Masjid demolition we witnessed Muslims acting as a monolith in a bid to defeat the Congress and the Bharatiya Janata Party. A decision had been taken by the voters to vote for any party best poised to defeat the BJP in particular. This is the response whenever Muslims feel their security to be under threat, perceived or otherwise. There is perhaps some truth in the allegation, that several Muslims too are now recognizing, of a vested interest having developed amongst so-called secular parties in promoting the perception of the community being under 'threat' to consolidate the minority vote.

Large-scale arrests of innocent Muslim youth across the country are a huge issue, which have had an impact even in states where no such detentions have been reported. The point being made is that economic growth and development becomes an overriding concern only when the Muslim voter feels a little secure, and able to take cognizance of his impoverished state in a dispassionate manner, without fear of his life. For when security is not an issue, the Muslim voter acts as an individual like anyone else, voting for his future and not against any particular party. For instance, in the 2012 Assembly elections in UP, or the earlier polls in Bihar,

Muslims voted for the party or parties they felt would work for their progress and development, while keeping them secure. The last is always in the periphery, the linkages firm in the Muslim mind. For instance, in Badaun, the Muslims gathered outside the Jama Masjid told me that they would vote for the Samajwadi Party but admitted that the sitting BJP candidate was popular. 'We just have to call him and he comes,' was the consensus. But they were clear they could not vote for him so long as he remained with the BJP, as the linkage between progress and development in their minds, and rightfully so, was that of security and peace.

Political parties, even those that describe themselves as secular, have often overplayed a threat to security to try and consolidate the Muslim vote behind them. This has worked well for the political class in the past, but not so any longer as most Muslims, even in UP and Bihar, have become wise to this ruse. This was one of the primary reasons why in both UP and Bihar, the political parties have had to campaign on the development platform, unable to stoke the fires of communalism and subsequent insecurity. The result is that all political leaders have had to state their position on issues concerning economic growth and development in recent days, to convince the Muslims that they were on the right track and no longer interested in exciting passions over non-existent threats.

Interestingly, Muslims might not vote for foreign policy, but it does have an impact on their psyche. There is a natural affinity for the Palestinians that seems more connected to Muslims now than before, because the Indian state has shifted far more towards the West, leaving such struggles in the realm of identity and secular politics in India. There is a strong dislike for Israel that cuts across classes in the Muslim community, and while the masses are not particularly vocal on such issues, Muslim organizations often join foreign policy initiatives against Israel.

A case in point, where even conservative outfits like the Jamaat-e-Islami joined the progressive and Left campaign, is the India-US civilian nuclear energy agreement initiated by then US President George W. Bush and Prime Minister Manmohan Singh. Muslim organizations came out in full strength to oppose this agreement, which they perceived as an instrument to settle India firmly on the US side. Post-9/11 developments had alienated the Muslim community across the world, Indians being no exception, with the result that India's attempt to strengthen strategic ties with the US on the latter's terms created considerable hostility amongst both the progressive and the conservative sections of Muslim society in India. Huge meetings opposing the agreement were held as the mullahs joined the secular and progressive political parties to denounce the agreement. But the fickleness of the Muslim conservatives was evident in the build up to the Assembly elections in West Bengal and Kerala, as the Jamaat-e-Islami and other such organizations quietly withdrew from the nationwide campaign, to direct their people to vote against the Left parties in both states.

A point of difference within the Muslim community in foreign policy is Saudi Arabia, whose Wahabi Islam has a good following amongst the conservatives. It is this lot that has changed the Persian greeting 'Khudahafiz' to 'Allahhafiz', used increasingly by conservative Muslims across India. This despite the fact that the first is a recognized greeting and in use in Iran, and the latter does not exist except as a forced substitute in India. Similarly, the Awadh greeting 'Adaab', sweet and informal and secular to the ears, has almost vanished from use being replaced by the more formal and in my view harsher, 'As-Salaam Alaikum'.

Liberal Muslims however, are critical of Saudi Arabia and join the progressive movement to question the large oil producers' close relations with the US, and its policy of exporting 'religion' to the world. As a resident editor, I was surprised to receive a call from the Saudi Arabian ambassador to India. An affable man who had once sent wine bottles to journalists on Diwali as a goodwill gesture, he extended me an invitation on behalf of the Saudi King to visit the country for Haj. I could not believe it, and told him that I would go like a shot if the invitation was to interview His Highness. The envoy was not amused and repeated the offer to which I replied, after racking my brains for a proper response, 'I am very grateful for the offer, but I am not ready to go for Haj as I have still to shed my responsibilities.' This worked pretty well, and I rang up an aunt to further confirm the propriety of the response. I got a big pat on the back and a surprised, 'how did you get it so right!'

Many in my family have gone for Haj and many more have not. My grandmother did, and returned overwhelmed by the human and not just the religious experience of the pilgrimage. A jovial cousin who accompanied his more devout wife for Haj returned with the story of her stoning the devil, and as she was pelting stones with all her might, an aggrieved voice (of the devil of course) said, calling her name, 'not you too….'. This had us guffawing for days after, while the elders in the family were amused but felt obliged to admonish our irreverence. I never realized how big an occasion it was for Muslims until my stint in politics, where I often observed the pomp and ceremony with which a potential Haji was seen off by entire families, believers who were sure that the Haj would bring peace and make a difference to their lives. One cannot say if it did, but then I have learned to respect those who follow their belief, so long as it is innocent and non-intrusive.

Saudi Arabia remains a close ally of the US despite its authoritarian religiosity, even as leaders like Muammar Gaddafi and Saddam Husain have been hunted down and killed in humiliating circumstances for far less. My brother, who was posted briefly in Saudi Arabia as a top executive in a multinational corporation, was shocked when on an extraordinarily hot day he saw a burkha-clad woman sitting in the back of a small truck in the boiling sun, while the passenger seat beside the driver in the air-conditioned cabin was empty. He pointed this out to his Saudi driver who shrugged off the question with a, 'well, her relationship with the man in the driver's seat is probably one where marriage is possible, so obviously she cannot sit beside him.' Backward laws, oppressive politics, and religiosity make up the Saudi Arabian mix. I remember when I wrote a series of articles on these lines I got any number of mails from Indian Muslims working there who applauded the articles, and whispered that they had been circulating these to others in that country. But then oil talks, and stops the US campaign against the Arabs and West Asians short of Saudi Arabia's shores.

Muslims, like all Indians, live with a multitude of interests, beliefs, passions and concerns. Like Indians, there are commonalities in responses, but often the views are totally divergent. Such as the responses to Pakistan in North India as compared to those from southern parts, where Muslims are more bothered about what is happening in Dubai and Qatar (where their relatives work), than in Islamabad.

Interestingly, there is little connect between the Indian Muslim and Jammu and Kashmir, with the plight of the Kashmiris never really an issue in Muslim households in the rest of India and vice versa. Two separate peoples, preferring to leave it that way. This is one of the reasons why successive governments have been able to get away with amazing levels of brutality and oppression in the Kashmir Valley. If the Muslims in UP and Bihar and other states of India had made this their cause and allowed it to influence their vote, the governments would have worked to bring some levels of justice and accountability in the Valley. Nothing works more for the politicians than the vote, and just as they run around like headless chickens promising everything from reservations to jobs to security before elections in any of the other states for the vote, they could have done the same for Kashmir if the people had connected and made a common cause of oppression and suffering.

This is an observation, but not a certainty. Because it could have worked the other way, and the Muslims outside Jammu and Kashmir might have found life more difficult as a result. The Urdu language is an example that supports this side of the argument. Urdu, despite being a language synthesizing the cultures and religions of India, came to be attached to the Muslim community after Independence. In the process of communalization, Urdu disappeared from the education network altogether. In states like UP where it was included as an election promise, the absence of Urdu teachers and textbooks killed it. The BJP governments in the states and at the centre presided over the extinction of Urdu by withdrawing advertisements from the fledgling Urdu media, which died as a result. Any number of newspapers closed down, with an entire generation entering adulthood without any knowledge of Urdu. It remains confined now to a few police stations in Punjab where old Sikh police officers still maintain their registers in the Urdu script. A beautiful language with a rich treasure of poetry and literature is thus on the verge of extinction.

Epilogue

Today, I first search for solace. I look for an assurance that there are people who still care. And that they are not from one community, but come from all the diversity that makes India. The space and the solace exist wherever people are speaking, not with religious identities but as Indians who care. Wherever there is an understanding that there is no 'other'—that there is only the 'we'. Since the solution cannot come from any 'one', it has to come from 'all'.

I do find solace. I see that space—diminished, under threat, fearful perhaps—but there. It is visible as a space not just for Muslims, or for Christians, or for Hindus, or for specific castes, but shines through the darkness as a space for all. Perhaps the numbers of people speaking have reduced drastically in the face of a worldview that seems to be ferociously devouring the foundation of freedom and rights on which India rests. As long as even a few remain, the many will follow, as Gandhi had so beautifully demonstrated. There is no future for India as we know it as a religious state; it can survive and grow only as a secular democracy. This is clearer today than it ever was, for me, as we confront this big challenge to our country's existence.

After this solace comes the realization that we built an India over the years where democracy was denied to all except a few. And where the masses—again not those of any one community but of all—never did get to pluck the fruits of equality, of rights, of justice, of development. Some saw the fruit, but from afar; others did not even know that they existed. And hence it was so very easy to deny them all that had been promised, to exploit them, and to refuse to let them become equal participants in the Idea of India. Really, this Idea never existed on the ground for the people struggling to cope, to make hardship acquire a meaning, to survive. So when it is taken away, the rights, the freedom, the essence of democracy is removed—as we now lament—the masses do not even realize it. How can they sense the loss of something they never had?

Religion thus becomes important: in a scenario where there is no square meal for the day, where the crops have failed, where there is no morrow....people turn increasingly to the gods to save them. In the process, all become more conservative, in every sense of the word, with the women, of course, bearing the brunt of this shift in ground. And then, if there is someone in our midst creating the 'other' as the one responsible for our plight, we find it easy to join in the targeting. Dalits were targeted like this as they were already at the bottom end of the ladder, so it was easy to mobilize caste prejudice against them.

I realize that Muslims are now the 'other' for similar reasons. Justification of course, can always be found. They are the largest minority community, and easily visible. Targeting them is equated with getting jobs, moving up the economic ladder, having better homes and, in short, getting rid of them realizes all dreams.

It is interesting that Muslims are now talking of what they can do to counter the hate. 'We have to introspect; what have we done wrong' is a refrain that I hear all the time now. Normally, I would have embraced this realization, as introspection is always good in a democracy. But today I find myself rejecting it completely, as this introspection comes from a defeatist posture, an acceptance of the propaganda of being the 'other', an almost desperate 'we will do anything, just please do not hurt us' attitude. It comes from fear.

What has the Indian Muslim done wrong? That s/he has not reformed personal laws, yes. That is an ongoing struggle from within. The Supreme Court is set to move on the abhorrent practice of triple talaq—not because of the government or a particular political party, but because of an organization of Muslim women, the Bharatiya Muslim Mahila Andolan, which has moved the courts for justice. There is a debate within the community on the issue and the BMMA case itself is a reflection of this.

Women—from every community—have been working on reforming personal laws and empowering their gender which, unlike minority communities, forms 50 per cent of the population and remains neglected and impoverished even today. Hindu women are struggling for equal property rights, Christian for equal marital rights amongst other issues. Marital rape is a concern for all.

It does not help the cause of women per se, when their laws are dragged into the realm of religious rights, whether by conservatives from their own religions, or by the government seeking to use the issue to further batter a community. The community—in this case the Muslims—responds by becoming more resistant to reform, turning the clock back for its women. It is ironic that those very persons who could not legislate 33 per cent reservation for women in Parliament and the state assemblies are so concerned about a personal law that impacts less than 1 per cent of the women of this country.

But insofar as politics is concerned, what has any Muslim done that s/he should be pilloried and hanged? Indian minorities vote for secular parties. They see themselves as being stakeholders in this democracy. They value the vote as much as anyone else. They are not terrorists; they are not militants; they do not work against India; they do not create communal violence; they just want to live in peace. They have demonstrated over these seventy years that they are Indians; that their present and their future lies here; that they are against violence; that they condemn terrorism. They, too, are citizens of India as defined in the Indian Constitution.

So I reject the current effort by some Muslims to introspect as a community, since the very premise is wrong, and hence the results of this thought process will be drastically wrong as well. Instead of feeding into a secular solution, it will hasten the exclusion of the community from larger processes. This is as stupid and futile as Indian Muslims jumping up every now and again to condemn acts of terror committed by foreign nationals! How are we responsible for what other misguided, fanatical Muslims in the world, be it Pakistan or Saudi Arabia, do? Yes we condemn it, as do all peace-loving citizens of the world, but certainly not as Muslims.

This is not to deny the need for introspection per se. But it has to be secular in spirit, by all. There can be no Hindu introspection or Muslim introspection; all who are concerned have to think together. Critically, honestly, we have to ask 'Where have we, as Indians, not as religious communities, gone wrong?' The answer might then, and then only, carry a solution.

The problem to me, lies in the secularism that India has followed. The word secular is not a problem, though I am aware that many are now becoming defensive about it because of aggressive attacks on the terminology. In fact, there is no substitute in the English language that carries the same wide connotations as secular. The problem lies in how we have understood it politically, and made it simply rhetoric, instead of turning it into action. This, to explain, will require another book, but suffice it to say that 2017 has exposed the holes in the concept of secularism that one had failed to recognize and take stock of. All that our governments in the past needed to do was to act for all the people equally, instead of singling out Muslims in rhetoric and doing nothing on the ground.

To give a simplistic example: if the governments since Independence had worked on a war footing to provide education and health facilities for all without exception, this would have been an inclusive response as per the tenets of the Indian Constitution. But by not doing so, and keeping Indians even in the twenty-first century without access to health and education, and by creating a dual system (one for the rich and another for the poor) the political system created anger and frustration. This anger was then directed at the minorities, when 15-point special packages for Muslims (always treated as a vote bank in the name of secularism) were announced on the eve of the elections, even though all other disadvantaged groups had been excluded from the benefits as well. Hence, even as one political party used these flaws to build a communal concept of the 'other' so perfectly, the others, claiming to be 'secular', ensured that the holes in the concept of secularism just kept getting bigger as they had lost the needle and the thread to sew them shut.

The solution to the challenges today has to come from within secularism. It is not just a word added to the Preamble of the Constitution, but needs to be a response that is inclusive and pluralistic in every sense of the word. It cannot come from communities sitting in their little holes trying to find out what went wrong. It has to come from the survivors of the recent upheaval as secular citizens of India, not as representatives of religion.

It is here that I see myself differ from many I know. Perhaps many liberal Muslims I know tend, in times of adversity, to shrink back into a comfort zone defined by the community. This is a natural response from a minority, more so a minority currently under threat. But it needs to be shed, as the logical conclusion of such an approach will strengthen the threat, not reduce it. Just as superstition can only be cut by rationality, communalism can only be defeated by secularism.

It's interesting that those believing in a communal ideology realize this, and hence the concerted attack on secularism as a term, as a 'Western' concept, and now as even 'anti-national'. For they know that it carries within it the antidote to the poison of hate and divisiveness and is the only weapon that can cripple communalism which thrives on these. Unfortunately, those who speak for secularism do not realize this. Many are looking at solutions through religious introspection and discourse, while others have become defensive about secularism, with many a liberal meeting over the past years hesitating to use the word and crying for the need to find another word. Why? Because those who are threatened by secularism are asking us to? They then have succeeded in doing precisely what they intended—if we drop it as a concept, then it has to be dropped from the Indian Constitution as well. And the consequences of that are crystal clear.

It is necessary for all of us to emerge from our spaces, to join hands, and to use all that we were taught to forge new alliances, to rectify mistakes jointly, and to look upon the challenges today as an opportunity to plug loopholes, and emerge from the exercise stronger, not weaker.

Muslims must learn to join the larger struggles for social justice, against discrimination and for social equity. Perhaps this is the one major mistake that the community made in the larger political arena, when it stayed away from the struggles of others also at the receiving end. Here I blame the post-Independence Muslim elite which, as a class, always looked out for its creature comforts and resisted the effort to participate in people's struggles, lest this place it outside the government patronage umbrella.

This patronage was another pacifier used by successive so-called secular governments to ensure that concern for the minorities remained confined to the accommodation of a handful of Muslim elites who were happily ensconced in high positions as figureheads of secularism. The elite thus became resistant to identifying itself with even the Muslim masses, whose lot, like that of all others, never did improve and, in fact, steadily worsened. In the process, the identification of the poor of one community with the poor of another was erased, keeping class out of secular struggles altogether. Today, the Muslim elite is finally expanding the contours of its limited understanding, but even so this remains confined to a shake of the head, with fear being the overriding emotion.

The Muslim intellectual has gone out of business. If you look around, s/he has little to say and is terrified of saying even that little. As during the time of the Shah Bano judgement, when Muslim women supporting the judgement could be counted on the fingers on one hand, today in face of the major challenge the Muslim elite has all but disappeared from view. Except for a handful of die-hards, there is little public response from the elite, which whispers its concerns in private rooms but is too terrified to speak publicly.

In times such as this, fundamentalists are more courageous, and can find their voices if push becomes shove. But this is exactly what India does not need. Fundamentalism of one stripe cannot be fought by fundamentalism of another, as this creates more hate, more violence and destruction.

The arguments used by the forces of divisiveness vary, according to the exigencies of time. In the 1990s a huge movement fuelling hate was organised by right-wing forces over the Babri Masjid issue as has been discussed earlier in the book. At the turn of the century these forces received a new fillip with the Gujarat massacres. Now the campaign has embraced different issues, all being turned into potent weapons generating violence, death, displacement. The targets remain the Dalits and the Muslims, the second being added to the first on a wide scale.

The 'love jihad' that had Muzaffarnagar burning in 2013 with thousands of Muslims fleeing for their lives, and ending up as persons displaced from the homes they have lived in for decades, continues even today. This was accompanied by the 'ghar wapsi' campaign that hit both Muslims and Christians on the conversion issue, with mobs roaming the districts of the North Indian states, particularly western Uttar Pradesh, attacking homes and churches based on wild accusations that conversations were taking place. Sporadic violence of the kind has always dotted the Indian landscape since Independence, but now in the twenty-first century this was for the first time given a plan, a campaign colour, and almost complete impunity from the law.

In the last two years these two issues that were used to strike terror in the Indian hinterland had another, even more lethal companion, with 'gau-rakshak' mobs roaming the streets and the highways. The first lynching that shocked India was that of Mohammad Akhaq in 2015 who was dragged out of his home by a mob and beaten to death on little more than suspicion, spread by the well-oiled rumour machinery of course, that he was storing beef. The forensic report cleared him and his family of the charge, but by then he was dead, and his son in hospital with serious injuries. The family till today is terrified, unable to return home, with charges against it for consuming beef still in force.

Dalits have also not been spared, with Dalit youth being caught by a mob in Una, Gujarat, tied, stripped and flogged in public view. Interestingly the vigilantes seem to be under instructions to film their own atrocity and put it on the social media, to ensure widerspread terror.

Since then beatings and lynchings of ordinary, innocent folk by cow vigilantes have become a norm. Pehlu Khan, returning from a cattle fair in Rajasthan with milch cows to his home in Haryana was stopped on the main highway by a crowd on motorcycles. He and his sons were seized, and beaten mercilessly with the old man being killed. Today his sons, badly injured with fractures and with not even an offer of help from the authorities are running from pillar to post to save themselves from the First Information Reports filed against them. The accused of course, have not been arrested. Men have been attacked for honking at a cow on the streets, for brushing against a cow while walking, as mob vigilantism spreads across the north belt of India. The assailants are no longer fearful, confident that the police is their protection.

It is clear that fundamentalism can only be fought by secularism. This weapon has to be honed, with all the rust of the past seventy years erased. In that struggle there is an opportunity, not just to win but to emerge with a better system that can withstand future challenges by ensuring the realization of the Idea of India.

India's secularism has to find new assertiveness to cope with the challenges posed by international war-mongering and internal divisiveness. It has to be matched by political understanding of her complex character, which embodies a pluralism that should be strengthened to breed unity and not exploited to turn on its own people.

To return to speaking personally, I find that all I was taught has sharpened this conviction about the importance of secularism, not weakened it. I remember my grandmother, Anis Kidwai, telling me when the Emergency imposed by Indira Gandhi was at its worst, 'this will not last, it cannot last; she will be defeated.' This was at the height of the Emergency when all dissent was being jailed, where the media had crawled, and there seemed to be no light at the end of the dark tunnel. My Nani, along with her close friends Subhadra Joshi and Mridula Sarabhai, had gone to meet Indira Gandhi to remind the then Prime Minister that she was Nehru's daughter. But all three freedom fighters had been turned away. So she had no straw to clutch, but perhaps she did not need one, as she spoke out of deep conviction, based on her unwavering Idea of India.

Acknowledgements

Acknowledgements are more difficult than it seems, as either these run into pages or crucial persons are forgotten. So I will focus on thanking the three persons who have made this book possible in more ways than one. Renuka Chatterjee of Speaking Tiger who was certainly not conventional in her approach, Ravi Singh who quietly gave the go ahead without fuss or discussion, and Shalini Krishan who came in last and was not just thorough in her editing but very patient with my stretched deadlines. Quiet, firm and polite, and very professional—my ideal publishing team!

www.ingramcontent.com/pod-product-compliance
Lightning Source LLC
Chambersburg PA
CBHW052050220426
43663CB00012B/2519